OSPREY/**AIRWAR** SERIES   EDITOR: MARTIN WINDROW

# GERMAN FIGHTER UNITS
## 1914-May 1917

### BY ALEX IMRIE

## COLOUR PLATES BY
## MICHAEL ROFFE
## AND G.A. EMBLETON

First published in Great Britain in 1978 by Osprey Publishing, Elms Court, Chapel Way, Botley, Oxford OX2 9LP, United Kingdom.
Email: info@ospreypublishing.com

ISBN 0 85045 290 2

Printed in China through World Print Ltd.

FOR A CATALOGUE OF ALL BOOKS PUBLISHED BY OSPREY MILITARY AND AVIATION PLEASE CONTACT:

Osprey Direct UK, PO Box 140, Wellingborough, Northants, NN8 2FA, UK.
Email: info@ospreydirect.co.uk

Osprey Direct USA, c/o MBI Publishing, PO Box 1, 729 Prospect Avenue, Osceola, WI 54020, USA.
Email: info@ospreydirectusa.com

www.ospreypublishing.com

Editor's note

This book is a facsimile edition of a title from Osprey's Airwar series, issued by Osprey to mark the 25th anniversary of Airwar's launch. When books in the Airwar series were first published, certain details were omitted as the information was not yet in the public domain. Although the information has since become available, readers should note that it has not been included in the reprinting of Airwar. The complete series has been re-issued as a set of commemorative historical documents, and we hope that you will enjoy it as such.

# FROM CARBINE TO MACHINE GUN

The two-seater units of the *Fliegertruppe* that went to war in August 1914 were attached to the Regular Corps and Army HQs for reconnaissance purposes. The Germans did not have a machine gun suitable for use in the air and their aircraft were unarmed except for the side-arms carried by the pilots and observers. During the deployment of forces in the West, and in the war of movement that followed, encounters with enemy aircraft were rare due to the small number of aeroplanes in use by each side and the large area of operations. This situation changed with the introduction of static warfare. The machines of the *Feldflieger Abteilungen* were then used for artillery co-operation as well as reconnaissance, and as a result, aerial activity became concentrated near the front lines.

The number of encounters with enemy aeroplanes increased and almost immediately the German units began to suffer losses from combats with machine gun armed 'pusher' aircraft. By early 1915 the German crew members' pistols had been supplemented with 25-shot carbines, and a small number of their aircraft were armed with captured weapons of the Hotchkiss and Lewis varieties positioned on makeshift mountings and fired from the observers' front seats. But encumbered by parts of the aircraft structure and restricted by the rotating propeller, their effectiveness was extremely limited. However, more powerful aero-engines being produced in Germany led to the development of suitable aeroplanes to carry machine guns. The provision of a light machine gun had been high on the priority list since the outbreak of war; the Parabellum LMG14 and the Bergmann LMG both appeared early in 1915, but production was slow and there remained an acute shortage of machine guns for aerial use until well into 1915.

Apart from arming the normal two-seater type of aircraft by changing the relative positions of pilot and observer, and providing the observer with a rotatable ring-mounted machine gun, attempts were made to produce aircraft with a machine gun firing forward in the flight direction. Two main approaches to the problem were made, both of which attempted to position the machine gunner in the nose of the aeroplane, allowing him an uninterrupted field of fire forward. Twin-engined and pusher types were produced, and early production versions of these two types of *Kampfflugzeuge* reached the front in June 1915. However, before they could be fully evaluated under operational conditions, the Fokker monoplane arrived on the Western Front.

A small single-seater wire-braced monoplane powered by an 80hp rotary engine, the Fokker was highly manoeuvrable and possessed the unique feature of a machine gun firing in the flight direction. The main difference between the Fokker and the other *Kampfflugzeuge* was that it was a single-engined tractor design and the gun was rigidly fixed to the machine, being aimed by flying the aircraft about its three axes. Only a few inches in front of the machine gun, a wooden propeller blade passed the muzzle approximately 2,400 times every minute, but due to an ingenious timing device, the bullets did not strike the propeller blades when the gun was firing.

The idea of getting machine gun bullets to pass between the blades of a revolving propeller was not new. Such an obvious advantage for a fighting aeroplane had been recognized before the war, and work had been done in England, France, Italy, Germany and Russia to find a solution to the problem. In most cases the poor quality of the ammunition then in use, with its high percentage of hang-fire rounds, made the successful development

3

of practical gun-gears even more difficult. It was for this reason that the Frenchman Raymond Saulnier discarded his synchronizing gear and fitted metal deflector wedges to the propeller blades to prevent the low number of hits noted when free-firing a machine gun through the arc of a wooden airscrew. Roland Garros, the famous pre-war aviator, knew of Saulnier's work, and after the outbreak of war continued to experiment with armoured propellers of the same type, eventually using this device operationally with some success. On 18 April 1915, Garros was brought down behind the German lines and captured. Although he burned his Morane Parasol Type L, the fire did not destroy the

armoured propeller and it was immediately obvious to the Germans how the 'System-Garros' worked.

In Germany, Franz Schneider, technical director and chief designer for LVG had devoted himself to the synchronization problem for a number of years. He patented his idea on 15 July 1913 but despite repeated requests to be allowed to undertake practical experiments, was prevented from doing so by the *Kriegsministerium*, even after the outbreak of war. Equally surprising was that full details of Schneider's patent were published on 30 September 1914 in *Flugsport* magazine. *Idflieg*, realizing the usefulness of the device used by Garros, immediately wanted to institute a similar system. During discussions with aircraft manufacturers on this matter, the amazing fact emerged that a mechanical synchronizing gun-gear was already in existence, ready for use, at the Fokker Aeroplanbau GmbH at Schwerin. Although there were differences between the Fokker synchronized gun-gear and the Schneider interrupter mechanism, it is

1. The Dutch designer Anthony Fokker posing with one of his E III monoplanes and wearing the ribbon of the Iron Cross second class in his buttonhole. The award was promised to him by the Feldflugchef if he could prove the practicality of firing a machine gun through a revolving propeller by bringing down an enemy aircraft using such a device.

considered that the Fokker gear was essentially based on the LVG (Schneider) patent.

Not only did Fokker have a gun-gear that worked, he also had a suitable aeroplane for its installation with a machine gun. He was given a Parabellum LMG14 which was installed on a Fokker M5K, and demonstrated before *Idflieg*, proving that the combination worked satisfactorily. The authorities however, were sceptical and felt that there was only one real way to prove the weapon. Fokker was ordered to take his machine to the front in order to demonstrate it to operational flying personnel, and while there to personally shoot down an enemy aeroplane with it. The award of the Iron Cross 2nd Class was promised by the *Feldflugchef, Major* Thomsen, if Fokker successfully obtained a victory.

Fokker arrived in the German V Army area on 23 May 1915 and flew the Fokker M5K/MG from Stenay aerodrome, the base of the V Army HQ two-seater unit. He was accompanied by *Leutnant* Parschau, an experienced pre-war military pilot who later shared the demonstration flying. Qualified rotary-engine pilots were allowed to fly the aircraft, and when conditions were suitable, Fokker himself undertook flights to the front looking for enemy aircraft, but did not find any inviting targets. The Fokker flying was closely watched by *Hauptmann* Haehnelt, the Staff Officer for Aviation (*Stofl*) of V Army. After days of

2. Leutnant Kurt Wintgens of Feldflieger Abteilung 67 in his Fokker monoplane (E 5/15) fitted with a Parabellum LMG 14 machine gun. Note the headrest, which it was thought would be necessary to ensure accurate aiming of the gun.

fruitless search, Fokker went north to VI Army where more enemy aerial activity was reported. Based again on the army HQ two-seater unit's aerodrome, Fokker continued his demonstrations before senior officers from the area, including *Hptm* Stempel, the *Stofl* of VI Army. Also quartered on this aerodrome at Douai was *Feldflieger Abteilung* 62, and it was to this unit that *Ltn* Oswald Boelcke and *Fähnrich* Max Immelmann belonged. Both were keen observers of the Fokker activity.

At Douai, Fokker waited for enemy aircraft to come across the front; since none materialized, a front patrol was carried out whereby Fokker was escorted to the lines by armed two-seater aircraft. This was also unsuccessful, and it has been recorded that Fokker received a severe fright from bursting anti-aircraft shells, the explosions of which could be heard above the low noise level of the Oberursel rotary engine. After this flight Fokker abandoned his attempts to bring down an Allied aeroplane and returned to Germany.

Possibly because of recommendations made by Haehnelt and Stempel, the authorities were aware of the potential of the Fokker monoplane and the type

5

went into series production. As output from the Schwerin factory allowed, aircraft were sent to the *Armee Flug Parks* of the various armies for distribution to front line units. By the end of July, 15 examples were flying on the Western Front. Their method of introduction was similar in all Army areas in that they were attached to the two-seater *Feldflieger Abteilungen*. It was considered that one fighting aeroplane of this type per unit would be sufficient to cover the limited requirement for escort and local defence although no tactics had been worked out for the operational use of the single-seaters. They were flown on a form of roving commission, by pilots who had also to perform their usual share of two-seater work. If enemy aircraft were reported the Fokkers would take off and search for them, often without success. In an attempt to keep the mechanics of the synchronized machine gun from the enemy, the use of the Fokker monoplanes was restricted to the airspace over and behind the German lines. Reluctance on the part of the Fokkers to cross the lines was wrongly interpreted by the Allies, who thought that the enemy pilots had 'cold feet'. But despite the potential of the Fokker monoplane, the majority of senior officers favoured the heavily armed twin-engined *Kampfflugzeug* approach to air-fighting, and by this time a number of these aircraft were

3. Unteroffizier Richard Dietrich of Feldflieger Abteilung 24 with his Fokker monoplane (E 6/15). The fuselage motif and the word Habicht (Hawk) is probably the earliest example of a personal marking applied to a fighter aeroplane. This aircraft is also Parabellum-armed, due to the shortage of the standard LMG 08/15.

attached singly to specially selected *Feldflieger Abteilungen*.

# INTO BATTLE

Anthony Fokker left his three demonstration machines, two Fokker E Is and an unarmed aircraft, believed to have been a Fokker M5K, at Douai when he returned home. Boelcke had flown rotary-engined Fokker two-seaters as early as December 1914 and had carried out practice flights on the E I shortly after Fokker arrived at Douai. On Fokker's departure Boelcke was allocated Fokker E 3/15 and flew this machine in addition to carrying out his two-seater duties. Immelmann, who lacked rotary engine experience, was greatly interested in the monoplanes but did not want to leave the front for a conversion course at Schwerin. But at the end of July, after familiarization flights with Boelcke, he did some flying in the unarmed machine, and took up the armed Fokker E I for the first time on 31 July, firing the machine gun at a ground target and obtaining two hits. Then, early in the morning of 1 August there was enemy air activity over Douai. Boelcke, airborne in E 3/15, engaged the enemy but was forced to break off his combat owing to a jammed machine gun. While Boelcke was in the air, Immelmann left the ground in E 13/15 and managed to force a B.E.2c to land despite experiencing trouble with his machine gun. This was Immelmann's first victory and probably the first scored by the Fokker monoplane, although there is reason to believe that *Ltn* Wintgens, a product of the Schwerin school, was flying such a monoplane in *Feldflieger Abteilung* 67 when he had a successful air combat with a Morane Parasol on 1 July.

Boelcke's first victory in the Fokker came on 19 August when he forced a British biplane to land just inside the Allied lines.

In the months that followed both Immelmann and Boelcke continued to have successful combats and the inclusion of their names in news communiqués made them the best known of all the early Fokker fighters. While these men were beginning to make a

4. Offizierstellvertreter Weckbrodt posing with the Fokker E I which he flew with Feldflieger Abteilung 58 on the Eastern Front during 1915. This pilot later served with Jagdstaffel 26 and was killed on 13 October 1917.

name for themselves around Douai, further north in the VI Army area Fokker monoplanes were being attached to other two-seater units. In anticipation of receiving such a machine, *Unteroffizier* Dietrich of *Feldflieger Abteilung* 24 carried out six circuits and landings in the Fokker belonging to *Feldflieger Abteilung* 5 at Wasquehal aerodrome on 24 August. Two days later he collected Fokker E 6/15, previously flown by *Obltn* Rodewaldt in *Feldflieger Abteilung* 9 from the *Armee Flug Park*. Initially Dietrich had to familiarize himself with the fixed machine gun and learn to clear jams quickly in the air. To provide air-firing practice he arranged for an aeroplane-shaped target to be laid out at a firing range near Seclin and found that diving attacks on this target usually resulted in bullet holes in his propeller. Judging by the number of wooden dowel repairs already made to the blades, it was obvious that the previous pilot had experienced similar trouble. After he had hit the propeller four times

Dietrich asked for it to be changed and as opportunity allowed between his reconnaissance flights he began patrols in the Fokker.

On 6 September, all the Fokker pilots in the Northern sector of VI Army area met at *Feldflieger Abteilung* 5 for discussions on aerial tactics and to assess the feasibility and value of formation flying. Present were Gelhorn and Nestler from *Abteilung* 5, Krefft from *Abteilung* 5b, and Dietrich. It was arranged that in the event of an enemy aircraft warning they would all meet over Lille and attack the enemy together.

The next day Dietrich had just returned from a two-hour reconnaissance flight over Bailleul-Merville-Estaires in the two-seater Albatros when an enemy formation was reported in the direction of

5. Leutnant Walter von Bülow of Feldflieger Abteilung 22 with Fokker E I 25/15. The twin-engined AEG in the background signifies the other approach to offensive air-fighting in vogue during the latter half of 1915. Several successful combats were undertaken by Leutnant Neubürger and Offizierstellvertreter Kossmahl in the machine shown.

Douai-Lille. Nestler, Krefft and Dietrich met as arranged at an altitude of 2,600 metres over Lille. They could see shell bursts in the direction of La Bassée and shortly afterwards made out the dark shapes of enemy aircraft amongst the cumulus clouds. There were four of them, two at the same height as the Fokkers and two about 600 metres above, apparently a reconnaissance and its escort. The German single-seaters were fairly spread out so a formation attack as they had planned was not possible. But over Carvin, Dietrich noticed a Hanriot monoplane turning in an easterly direction. He closed with this machine, caught it between Orchies and Marchiennes and opened fire. At the same moment the enemy fired back and made a steep left turn, narrowly missing the attacking Fokker. Dietrich followed the enemy and tried to get him in his sights again, but the Hanriot continued to circle and fire at the Fokker. A backward glance told Dietrich that the Vickers escort was diving towards him, and since his gun had jammed he broke off. Having cleared the jam, Dietrich chased after the enemy machines and managed to get within range of the Hanriot almost over the lines near Lens. After a few rounds his gun stopped again and he had to finally break off the fight.

On 26 September while engaged in an air-fight over Wattignies at a height of 2,300 metres, Dietrich experienced a carburettor fire. Deadstick he managed to reach the boundary of his aerodrome, and landed in rough ground, breaking the undercarriage and the propeller. The Fokker was dismantled and taken to the *Armee Flug Park*, but there was little chance of a replacement aircraft, as supply from Germany was then very limited. Dietrich resigned himself to two-seater work since he was 'basically a reconnaissance pilot anyway'.

The sparse distribution of single-seaters within this area is shown by the accompanying allocation list for VI Army dated 14 October 1915. (VI Army front extended over a distance of approximately 80kms)

| | | |
|---|---|---|
| *Abteilung* | 5 | Fokker E 9/15 |
| *Abteilung* | 5b | Fokker E 12/15 |
| *Abteilung* | 62 | Fokker E 13/15 and 37/15 |
| *Abteilung* | 2b | Fokker E 49/15 |
| *Abteilung* | 13 | Fokker E 3/15 |
| *Abteilung* | 9 | Fokker E 32/15 |

No single-seaters are listed as belonging to the remaining two-seater units of VI Army on this date. (*Abteilungen* 18, 4b and 24.)

The early successes of Immelmann and Boelcke apparently justified the allocation of two Fokkers to *Abteilung* 62, but that there was displeasure with this 'favouritism' is reflected in a letter from Immelmann on 11 September 1915, when he wrote: 'All the *Feldflieger Abteilungen* have a Fokker, we are the only unit with two. There is much jealousy since some units have crashed their Fokker in the meantime, while ours remain undamaged. Some units have asked why we have two Fokkers and *Stofl* 6 (*Hauptmann* Stempel) has told them that the Fokker has never been in such good hands as with *Abteilung* 62.'

In the original distribution of Fokker monoplanes within an army area, units flying for Army HQ (*Armee-Ober-Kommando—AOK*) and Regular Corps HQs invariably received a Fokker before any were assigned to units flying for Reserve Corps HQs. The manner of single-seater allocation in II Army illustrates this priority system.

The northern edge of II Army area was adjacent to the southern boundary of that of VI Army near Gommecourt, and extended almost 100kms to the south to Ribécourt, straddling the Somme river. This was an area of considerable aerial activity, and the single-seaters that appeared, singly at first then in number, to challenge the enemy were the forerunners of what became elite fighting units. In July 1915 *Abteilung* 23, the unit flying for II Army HQ at Roupy Lager, was awaiting the delivery of a Fokker monoplane. *Ltn* Berthold, a senior pilot of the unit, suggested that this machine should be flown by *Ltn* Buddecke, who although recently joined, had had experience on a similar type of monoplane before the war. Berthold collected and ferried from Germany the first AEG twin-engined G type machine to be allocated to II Army. It was decided to house this machine (G 21/15) in the grounds of nearby Château Vaux, which possessed a large field with good approaches providing a natural aerodrome. Berthold flew many bombing expeditions in the AEG but complained of its unsuitability for air-fighting.

At the beginning of September a Fokker E I was delivered and was also housed at Château Vaux. There was little interest in the Fokker, and it was looked upon almost as a toy, despite the successes of Immelmann and Boelcke. No definite ideas about the tactical use of the Fokker had yet been formulated and there was still much support for the large, heavily-armed *Kampfflugzeug* of which Berthold's AEG was an example.

Buddecke had his Fokker for three weeks before he encountered an enemy aircraft. On 19 September he took off from Vaux and engaged an R.E.5 at an altitude of 2,000 metres south of St Quentin. In the ensuing combat, the British pilot was killed and the machine, hit 108 times by Buddecke's fire, was landed by the observer. Shortly after this initial victory *Ltn* von Althaus joined the establishment with a second Fokker monoplane; both Fokkers and the AEG were kept in a large wooden hangar that had been built in the grounds of the château. This small contingent, with its complement of six officers and 30 men, was still a part of *Feldflieger Abteilung* 23 despite its isolation from the main unit.

Berthold wrote off his AEG during a landing on 15 September, but a few days later he collected another machine (G 26/15) from Germany. In this aircraft he had an air-fight with a British pusher biplane on 2 October which resulted in the deaths of his two observers. This proved to Berthold the complete unsuitability of the AEG for air-fighting and henceforth he devoted himself to the single-seater. In the meantime, Buddecke had brought down another enemy aircraft, a B.E.2c which had taken no less than 212 hits, some of which may have come from the gun of *Ltn* von Althaus' Fokker which had dived on the stricken machine and fired on it while Buddecke flew alongside waiting for the British aircraft to land. Buddecke's third victory, another B.E.2c, landed intact despite the accuracy of his shooting. In December Buddecke was transferred to the German Military Mission in Turkey and his Fokker E III was taken over and flown by Berthold.

In the northern part of II Army area, *Abteilung* 32, flying for XIV Reserve Corps, had been based on an aerodrome near Cambrai since 19 October 1914. Owing to its location, the unit had been exposed to the high level of aerial activity that the area fostered, gradually becoming involved in increasing numbers of air combats during 1915. As late as mid-August the bulk of the unit's work was still

**6. Leutnant Lörzer of Feldflieger Abteilung 25 about to take off in Fokker E I 20/15. Lörzer became a very successful fighter pilot with 44 confirmed victories, and was destined to reach high rank in a later Luftwaffe.**

7. A Fokker E I being flown by Leutnant von Althaus of Feldflieger Abteilung 23.

about 600 metres and I opened fire; fire was immediately returned by the enemy aircraft. I was about 200 metres higher than the enemy, so I descended firing all the time until I was about an aeroplane length behind him. I then saw that the pilot had been hit and the machine began to swing from side to side. Up to this time I was being fired at by the enemy's machine gun. I then flew into the enemy aircraft's slipstream and experienced a bad bump that threw my machine on its side and caused me to slip and lose 150 metres of height. I came out of the dive and tried to cut the enemy machine off from the front, but he was already in a steep dive which became vertical in the last 300 metres. The aeroplane was completely wrecked and both occupants of the B.E. biplane were killed.

being carried out on B category machines and only one machine-gun-armed aircraft was on strength. Despite this serious lack of firepower it was not until early in November that a Fokker monoplane was allocated to the unit. Unfortunately *Ltn* Leffers wrote-off this machine on its ferry flight when, during landing, lateral control became restricted due to the machine gun operating cable fouling an obstruction on the left side of the cockpit. A replacement Fokker was obtained from *Feldflieger Abteilung* 27 and Leffers brought this machine to the unit on 11 November. The previous day *Oblt* von Althaus had arrived with his Fokker on a ten-day detachment from *Abteilung* 23, but despite several patrols during this period, he did not encounter any enemy aircraft. One month after his abortive ferry flight with the first Fokker, *Ltn* Leffers had a successful combat, and filed the following report:

> On 5 December 1915 at 12.50 I took off from Vélu aerodrome in my Fokker single-seater E III 84/15. Around three o'clock I found myself over Bapaume and saw an enemy aeroplane almost over Martinpuich flying north at a height of 1,500 metres being shelled by our artillery. I immediately gave chase. Between Grévillers and Achiet-le-Grand I had closed to

Having Fokkers so widely dispersed throughout each army area meant that in the event of enemy penetrations no plans could be made for the efficient concentration of the machines available. The *Stofl* of the various armies were well aware of this shortcoming and late in 1915, depending on the tactical situation, the allocation of Fokker monoplanes was made more carefully. Soon single-seaters were grouped together for special operations, a move that proved the real value of the fighters. In a redistribution of single-seaters, some *Feldflieger Abteilungen* lost their Fokker allocation, while others, usually the two-seater units flying for the army HQs, had as many as four single-seaters attached, more than their normal establishment. The Fokkers were soon joined by a similar machine made by the Pfalz *Flugzeug-Werke* GmbH, but its production rate was considerably lower than that of the Fokkers, and at the end of 1915 out of a total of 107 single-seater fighting machines at the front, only 21 were Pfalz monoplanes.

Initially, the only air fighting tactics the Germans employed were those of finding an enemy aircraft and getting within range to shoot it down; single ill-armed enemy aircraft such as the Morane Parasol and the B.E.2c were easy meat for a well-flown Fokker monoplane. Even when escorted by another machine, the advantage usually remained with the Germans. As more single-seaters became available and the pilots became better practised, improved tactics evolved which increased the effectiveness of the fighter element—a fact reflected in the heavy toll of Allied aircraft taken during the last months of 1915.

Eight pilots who had scored victories on the Fokker monoplane by the end of the year were destined to receive Germany's highest military decoration, the *Pour le Mérite*, as their successes at air fighting grew. They were:

| | |
|---|---|
| *Oblt* Freiherr von Althaus | *Abteilung* 23 |
| *Ltn* Oswald Boelcke | *Abteilung* 62 |
| *Ltn* Buddecke | *Abteilung* 23 |
| *Ltn* Walter von Bülow | *Abteilung* 22 |
| *Ltn* Max Immelmann | *Abteilung* 62 |
| *Ltn* Gustav Leffers | *Abteilung* 32 |
| *Ltn* Kurt Wintgens | *Abteilung* 67 |
| *Ltn* Otto Parschau | *Kampfgeschwader* 1 |

Most Allied reconnaissance flights were now being contested and in this worsening situation, British records indicate that despite persistent effort few results were being obtained by December. On the 19th, there were almost 50 fights in the air, one of which ended with *Ltn* Parschau bringing down a B.E.2c at Oostkamp near Brugge; *Ltn* Leffers scored his second victory on 29 December when he shot down another B.E.2c at Marquion; *Ltn* Hess of *Feldflieger Abteilung* 62 started his score on 5 January 1916, the same day as Boelcke scored his seventh victory. A Morane was brought down by *Oblt* Schilling from *Abteilung* 5 on 10 January, while on 12 January Boelcke and Immelmann each claimed another victory.

Allied air losses brought about changes in RFC tactics in order to obtain reconnaissance information, as shown in the following quotation from *War in the Air*, the official history:

'We were now paying a heavy price in the endeavour to get on with our work. It was obvious that if the long reconnaissances which the army required were to be done at all, there must, pending the arrival of the new fighting squadrons, be a revision in tactics.

8. Fokker fodder: a wrecked B.E.2c from No. 12 Squadron Royal Flying Corps flown by Lt Gordon-Smith. It was brought down near Brugge on 19 December 1915 by Leutnant Parschau (extreme right in centre group) as his second victory.

This was made in an order issued from Flying Corps HQ on the 14 January 1916, which brought about, at a stroke, one of the drastic changes in the air war and crystallized the effects of the whole Fokker dominance—formation flying. The order read:

Until the Royal Flying Corps [is] in possession of a machine as good as or better than the German Fokker it seems that a change in the tactics employed becomes necessary. It is hoped very shortly to obtain a machine which will be able to successfully engage the Fokkers at present in use by the Germans. In the meantime, it must be laid down as a hard and fast rule that a machine proceeding on reconnaissance must be escorted by at least three other fighting machines. These machines must fly in close formation and a reconnaissance should not be continued if any of the machines become detached. This should apply to both short and distant reconnaissances. Aeroplanes proceeding on photographic duty any considerable distance east of the line should be similarly escorted. From recent experience it seems that the Germans are now employing their aeroplanes in groups of three or four, and these numbers are frequently encountered by our aeroplanes. Flying in close formation must be practised by all pilots.'

# SINGLE-SEATER SPECIALISTS

Within the various armies the grouping of several single-seaters on one aerodrome was known as a *Kampfeinsitzer-Kommando* (*KEK*). These were semi-permanent formations, the pilots and aeroplanes remaining part of their own *Feldflieger Abteilungen*, units being formed and dissolved according to the prevailing tactical situation. Some formations existed for a short period only, while others remained in operation for several months.

The effectiveness of the single-seater depended greatly on the enthusiasm and ability of the pilots, and although by early 1916 many of these men were still two-seater pilots, they were beginning to specialize in the recently formulated tactics of the fighter aeroplane.

Certain pilots were still introduced to the Fokker monoplane at the manufacturer's school at Schwerin, but to cater for the conversion of the bulk of the stationary-engine pilots a unit was formed at Mannheim in August 1915, designated *Kampfeinsitzer-Abteilung* 1. It was soon turning out

9. In order to get airborne as soon as possible, pilots on standby duty had to be near their aeroplanes, which meant that temporary accommodation was necessary on the aerodrome. Shown here are the three Fokker pilots of Feldflieger Abteilung 62 taking their midday meal in the readiness hut at Douai, early in January 1916. They are (left to right) Leutnants Hess, Boelcke and Immelmann.

a steady flow of pilots for the ever-increasing number of single-seaters in use at the front. *Vizefeldwebel* Wolff was a typical product of the Mannheim unit; he undertook his first operational flight on a Fokker on 31 January 1916, a 'barrage' patrol flying with *Feldflieger Abteilung* 34 from Cunel aerodrome in V Army area. Notes that he made provide an insight into the physical tasks involved in flying a Fokker monoplane:

> In the air one has to control the rpm of the engine; also the altimeter has to be monitored. Soon after take-off the compass has to be checked, and then the machine gun has to be tried by firing a few shots. These procedures take a little time, especially when the beginner tries the gun three times like I did. In addition, so that one is always ready for combat, the pilot must keep the gravity fuel tank full. Since this only contains about 20 litres of petrol it is more or less a constant job. After some 10 litres have been consumed, one pumps fuel every 15 minutes from the main tank which holds 100 litres. I found myself pumping about eight times an hour. All these duties are supposed to take only a few seconds to perform, but I was busy with them every few minutes, in any case oftener and longer than was really necessary . . . and my main task of course, was to look for enemy aircraft. To see them first and attack them by surprise was the ambition of all fighting pilots. I must admit however, that I attached less importance to this duty than to the fear that I myself would be surprised. Despite carrying out turns to watch the airspace behind me I made constant use of my rear-view mirror.

In the KEK pilots were not only under the command of the *Führer* of the *Feldflieger Abteilung* flying for the army HQ to which they were attached, but were also directly under the orders of that HQ and their operational usage was advised upon by the *Stofl* himself. It was this rigid control of the single-seaters, possibly more than their use in numbers, that improved their effectiveness so markedly. Although there was no official warning system, a start was made under AOK command, at increasing the time available between getting the single-seaters airborne and the arrival of enemy aircraft in the area.

Information on the height, strength and direction of enemy aeroplanes crossing the front generally originated with the forward Flak units, and by requesting that these details be relayed without delay to the army HQ it was an easy matter to pass them on to the AOK aerodrome. Single-seaters at readiness then started up and took off to intercept the enemy. The high percentage of interceptions that resulted in enemy aircraft being brought down by means of this procedure far outstripped the success of the earlier attempts with individual aircraft, where a pilot was often given inaccurate information on the position of enemy aeroplanes before taking off.

At Château Vaux during January 1916 more Fokker E IIIs became available and the establishment was increased to five machines. This formation, coming directly under the orders of II Army HQ, was named *Eindecker-Kommando-Vaux* on 11 January and was commanded by *Oblt* Berthold.

On 2 February *Oblt* von Althaus and Berthold each brought down a Voisin biplane near Chaulnes,

10. Fokker E III machines of Kampfeinsitzer-Kommando-Vaux, early in 1916. The leader of this temporary unit, Oberleutnant Berthold, is standing with his three mechanics by the nearest aircraft (E III 411/15).

and these were followed by a B.E., forced down by Berthold on 5 February between Grevillers and Irles. This B.E. was one out of two formations of four aircraft each that passed over the *Feldflieger Abteilung* 32 aerodrome at Bertincourt at about 10

11. Oberleutnant Student of III Army Fokkerstaffel taking off from Leffincourt aerodrome in his E III. Student later became Staffelführer of Jagdstaffel 9, and commanded the German paratroop force in World War II.

12. Pfalz E monoplane in flight; these were not nearly as popular as the Fokker machines of the same configuration, and the maximum number in use at the front was 56 at the end of April 1916.

am. Although the three single-seaters based there took off, they were unable to engage the British formations because of insufficient warning. Berthold, based further south at Château Vaux, and warned via the afore-mentioned AOK system, was able to gain height and have a successful combat.

On 7 February the strength of the fighter element in *Feldflieger Abteilung* 32, which was later to be named *Kampfeinsitzer-Kommando-Nord*, was as follows:

| *Ltn* Leffers | Fokker E III | 84/15 |
| *Ltn* Lehmann | Fokker E III | 400/15 |
| *Ltn* Rouselle | Pfalz E I | 220/15 |
| *Ltn* Diemer | Fokker E III | 440/15 |

On 20 February, on receipt of information that four enemy aircraft were in the air in the direction of Cambrai, the three Fokkers were dispatched. In the resulting combat *Ltn* Leffers brought down a B.E. biplane in flames at Aizecourt-le-Bas while *Ltn* Lehmann experienced a jammed machine gun that could not be cleared in the air and he had to give up the fight and return to the aerodrome.

Five enemy aircraft appeared over the aerodrome at around 1 pm on 5 March. Two bombs were dropped but did no damage. The three Fokkers immediately took off and gave chase; a difficult air fight followed without success. The value of the instructions contained in the Royal Flying Corps HQ order of 14 January is confirmed by the report that *Ltn* Lehmann made after this fight:

I took off at 12.47 to attack five B.E. aircraft which were flying in an easterly direction. I climbed above the enemy machines, as I flew a wide arc over Bapaume, and did not at first overhaul them. Meanwhile the enemy aircraft left the area of Cambrai in a north westerly direction towards Arras. I then dived on the formation and caught them up. As I dived and was about to fire another Fokker that was already in combat with the enemy flew across my line of sight and as a result I was forced to turn away in a steep turn. The range between the enemy formation and myself now increased. The other Fokker then dived on the furthest left B.E. and I attacked the others which remained in close formation. As I closed to about 200 metres, I opened fire on the lowest machine. The other Fokker turned away, and as I could see some anti-aircraft shells bursting close above me, I assumed that we had already crossed the front lines. The last phase of the fight had in fact taken place close to the front, but due to thick clouds it was not possible to pinpoint the exact location. During this fight I made the following observations. The [enemy] squadron seemed well practised against attacks from Fokkers. The aircraft kept close together at slightly different heights. Each aircraft could as a result, easily fire to the side and rear without endangering the other machines in the formation. In this way we were continually under fire from more than one aeroplane. The enemy also began his concentrated defensive fire as early as 500 to 600 metres range, [as] could be seen from the muzzle flashes. If we attacked one machine, the highest leading aircraft swung round to the rear to attack us, and when a machine dropped very much below the formation in combat, the rest of the enemy aeroplanes followed it down to defend it. The attacked aircraft then carried out rapid turns to avoid our fire, and this was successful since we could not follow these quick movements; the machines not under attack then turned in the same manner as the attacked machine. The speed of the enemy aeroplanes appeared to me to be higher than normal: also their rate of climb was very high. In general I obtained the impression that the British were not trying to get out of the way of the Fokkers, as they have done previously, but were rather using all their skill and energy to defend themselves.

The introduction of fighter formations in other army areas followed a similar pattern to that described for II Army and single-seater elements began to emerge along the whole length of the Western Front from the Belgian coast to the Swiss border. One of the southern units was *Kampfeinsitzer-Kommando-Habsheim* based near Mülhausen for the protection of nearby industrial installations from bombing attacks. A member of this unit was *Uffz* Ernst Udet, and on 12 March 1916, he was airborne in his Fokker to intercept a French Caudron which had been reported crossing the front line. Climbing through the overcast, Udet saw the enemy machine coming towards him and as the distance closed he was amazed to see that the enemy did not turn away from the path of the Fokker. He was even more amazed when he found that he did not have the courage to press the firing lever on his control column. As the aircraft passed each other, the French observer fired at the Fokker and Udet could feel bullets hitting his machine. Suddenly a glancing blow tore off his goggles. Instinctively the German dived for the protection of the cloud layer and felt the warm wetness of blood on his face caused by glass splinters from his broken goggles. Sick with fright and disgust, he was grateful that no one had witnessed his cowardice.

Six days after his Caudron affair, Udet was airborne to intercept what was reportedly two enemy aircraft. As he climbed towards Altkirch he saw a loose formation of Caudron, Farman and Voisin types—23 aeroplanes! He climbed above this armada, and placed himself in an ideal position for

attack. It was then that the hesitation that he had known before began to return: almost against his will, Udet forced his Fokker into a steep dive at the nearest Farman. Having taken the plunge, he approached the enemy at full throttle, firing from very close range. Bullets hit his machine as the enemy observers brought their guns to bear. Suddenly the enemy aircraft faltered, a blue flame shot from its exhaust pipe and it began to emit white smoke. A second later the Farman burst into flames. Udet dived away, levelled out about 360 metres below, and saw the blazing machine hurtle past, leaving a trail of black smoke. Even as he watched,

13. Vizefeldwebel Ernst Udet of Kampfeinsitzer-Kommando-Habsheim with his Fokker E III. Known locally as the 'Vosges Sparrow' at this time, Udet finished the war as the second highest scoring German fighter pilot with 62 confirmed victories.

15

14. In this collection of wrecked Allied aircraft can be seen the remains of Major F. E. Waldron's Morane Bullet Type N(A' 175). Waldron, who was the CO of No. 60 Squadron RFC, was brought down near Epinoy by Unteroffizier Howe in a Fokker monoplane of Feldflieger Abteilung 5 at 9.24 am on 3 July 1916.

the observer detached himself from the machine and fell froglike out of the sky with legs and arms outstretched. At that moment Udet did not think of the Farman's crew as human beings: he was conscious only of victory. It was the first of 62 successful aerial combats that he would engage in during the next 20 months.

During the winter battles in the Champagne a temporary grouping of seven Fokker monoplanes was made in III Army area on an improvised aerodrome at Monthois, south of the HQ at Vouziers. These aircraft were to provide patrol flights to prevent French reconnaissance of German preparations for a counter-attack aimed at straightening the line near Tahure. It was probably the success of the Tahure patrol system that led to V Army preparing a massive *sperre*—blockade—for the Verdun operation.

Initially, the single-seaters collected in V Army area were used for intensive patrol work, and it was to facilitate their management that they were

15. Following the loss of Immelmann on 18 June 1916, Boelcke was taken off operational flying duties and undertook an official mission to Turkey and other fronts. The serious aerial situation on the Somme brought about his return to the Western Front, where he formed Jagdstaffel 2 at Bertincourt on 27 August. He is seen here (left) with Oberleutnant Buddecke enjoying some yachting at Smyrna, during his tour of the Near East in July 1916.

grouped into assemblies of from ten to 12 aeroplanes. On the left side of the river Meuse *Kampfeinsitzer-Kommandos* were based on aerodromes at Avillers and Jametz flying for *Maasgruppe Ost*, while on the right *Maasgruppe West* had fighters flying from Cunel aerodrome, with further support on the right flank from III Army single-seaters based at Vouziers.

It had been thought that single-seaters were the most suitable type of aircraft for these patrols, but despite the concentration achieved, insufficient numbers were available at Verdun to be effective. Two-seaters from the *Kampfgeschwadern* were thus used to supplement the Fokkers, and eventually the bulk of the patrol work was done by these armed machines. But it was found that even when patrols were mounted in considerable strength the two-seaters could not prevent the intrusion of French reconnaissance machines. The fighters were then used to attack enemy penetrations, and it was in

their pursuit and attack of 'blockade breakers' that they obtained temporary superiority over the German lines.

The initial misuse of the single-seaters at Verdun, where they were tied to a patrol system which devoured flying hours and wore out engines, had in fact robbed them of their superiority as fighter aeroplanes. This failing was quickly pointed out by Boelcke, who complained that Jametz aerodrome was too far removed from the front, and obtained Haehnelt's permission to use a forward aerodrome initially with two, later three, aeroplanes. Boelcke chose his own aerodrome, a meadow near the village of Sivry, situated 11kms from the front. Once he was established at Sivry, Boelcke arranged for a forward observation post to telephone his aerodrome with details of enemy aerial activity in the area, a system which was a direct forerunner of the *Flugmeldedienst*. By this simple expedient Boelcke was able to remain on the ground until he received information that enemy aircraft were approaching the lines. He was thus able to conserve his forces, and more especially the serviceability of his

16. Newly arrived Fokker D Is of Jagdstaffel 1. At the end of October 1916 there were 74 aircraft of this type at the front, but they were a continual source of trouble due to their flimsy structure and poor workmanship, and were removed from operational status in December. Lack of directional stability made it necessary to retro-fit fins in front of the typical Fokker-shaped rudders.

aeroplanes, for actual combat flying. There was no stable organization for the assembled fighters at Verdun, but mainly through Boelcke's appraisal of the situation, Haehnelt was able to wield the KEK into fighting units and offset somewhat the increasing numerical superiority of the French. Boelcke's 'Sivry *Kommando*' was a good example of what a well-organized fighter unit should be. It produced results because of a number of factors: close proximity to the front, immediate reception of accurate information on enemy dispositions, a round-the-clock readiness during the hours of daylight, and a high morale with a keen fighting spirit amongst its members, due without doubt to Boelcke's personality and his own fine offensive spirit.

17

17. Leutnant Wintgens of Jagdstaffel 1 in his Halberstadt D II. Killed in action on 25 September 1916, he had 20 victories in aerial combat.

18. Hauptmann Buddecke and Rittmeister von Althaus watch while Oberleutnant Höhndorf of Jagdstaffel 4 prepares for flight. Note the ladder for cockpit access. The Halberstadt D II is in flying position with engine running. Château Vaux aerodrome, autumn 1916.

An insight into the conditions obtaining at Sivry were recorded by an NCO pilot who came to V Army in mid-1916. Due to some unfortunate incidents involving NCO single-seater pilots early in 1916, *Hptm* Haehnelt did not conceal his preference for fighter pilots of officer rank. However a shortage of officer candidates compelled him to circulate all units stating that suitable NCO pilots were required for training on single-seaters. It was this circular that prompted *Vizefeldwebel* Holler, a pilot in *Feldflieger Abteilung* 1, to volunteer. He attended a conversion course at Cologne with his mechanic to learn the handling characteristics and technical details of the Fokker monoplane. After approximately 20 flights Holler was passed out and returned to his unit, to find orders to proceed to the *Fokkerstaffel* at Jametz. On arrival there he requested the transfer of his mechanic, a move actioned within three days.

Holler was allocated a Fokker E III, which bore the figures '500' sand-blasted into the aluminium motor cowling. Although obviously a jubilee machine, its performance was disappointing, especially when compared to the other aircraft in the unit, which were of the later E IV type. Holler's aircraft climbed reasonably well to 2,000 metres but that was almost its ceiling. It was not possible for Holler to get a better machine by service merit and considerable coolness was shown him by the other pilots, even those of NCO rank, since he was the only non-officer aspirant in the unit. All the other pilots dined in the officers' mess while Holler ate with the men.

On 27 June *Fokkerstaffel* Jametz amalgamated with the Sivry *Kommando* to form a completely self-contained unit of six Fokker monoplanes designated *Fokkerstaffel* Sivry, intended to be fully operational by 30 June under the command of Boelcke. However, following the loss of Immelmann on 18 June, the High Command decreed that Boelcke should be forbidden to continue operational flying until further notice. He was given six weeks' leave of absence and ordered to undertake a tour of the other war theatres.

*Ltn* von Hartmann was given command of the unit and he retained some of the measures instituted by Boelcke at Sivry. Holler was pleased with the messing arrangements, since at Sivry all pilots used the officers' mess regardless of rank. The day was divided into four periods of readiness for the pilots, every fifth day being free of duty. Following this, one had the fourth readiness (1700 to dusk); on the second day came the third readiness period; on the third day the second period, and the fourth day the first readiness (dawn to 0900). The remainder of the fourth day and the off-duty time on the first day meant that in effect pilots had two complete days free of duty.

Despite E category aircraft delivery being restricted by the slow production of rotary engines—which reached a maximum of 20 per month—from June 1915 until April 1916, 180 single-seater fighter aircraft were introduced to front-line units. The two main failings of the armament fitted to these machines have already been mentioned: stoppages that could not be cleared easily in the air and synchronization trouble that resulted in bullets striking the propeller. These faults were never completely eradicated even on later types of fighter

19. Leutnant Kissenberth of Feldflieger Abteilung 9b flying his Fokker D II (540/16) over Colmar. Kissenberth's unit, Kampfeinsitzer-Kommando-Ensisheim, was re-designated Jagdstaffel 16 on 1 November 1916.

aircraft fitted with more sophisticated synchronization gun-gears. Their high frequency of occurrence on E category monoplanes fitted with Fokker *Gestänge Steuerung* (Pushrod Control) considerably reduced these machines' fighting potential. Although the Fokker monoplane was an outstanding weapon for its time, its technical superiority was not the main reason for its success. It gained fame on both sides of the lines because of the results obtained by a relatively small number of pilots, and this gave a false impression of its effectiveness to the German High Command.

Experienced pilots knew that a lightly loaded biplane fighter would give them better manoeuvrability in the sustained tight turns and improved rates of climb that were now needed to combat aircraft like the D.H.2 and the Nieuport, which were being encountered in ever-increasing numbers. The views of front line pilots were given sympathetic hearings by their *Stofl*, but the decisions on production orders were being made by senior officers who were really no longer completely familiar with the rapidly changing requirements of air-fighting in the spring and early summer of 1916. Both Boelcke and Berthold, amongst others, asked for single-seater biplanes early in 1916.

Time was certainly lost by the German aircraft manufacturers in trying to extract the maximum performance from rotary-engined wing-warping E category monoplanes. Both the Fokker E IV and the Pfalz E IV had poorer manoeuvrability than the types that had preceded them, and also a marked falling off in rates of climb above altitudes of 3,000 metres. Technical officers of the *Flugzeugmeisterei* were aware of the shortcomings of the E types and aircraft manufacturers were asked to devote themselves to solving the problem. Albatros, Fokker and Halberstadt brought single-seater fighter biplanes to the pre-production stage fairly rapidly, but for various reasons orders for these machines in number were not given as promptly as was expected. As a result, when the battle of the Somme began, the bulk of the single-seaters were still Fokker monoplanes.

The prolonged existence of a *Kampfeinsitzer-Kommando* in a given area showed a standing requirement for such a unit and it invariably assumed a semi-permanent status. This benefited pilots on attachment, as they tended to be based with the formation for a longer period, which improved their operational experience. A change in status can normally be identified by a change in nomenclature as units usually became known as *Kampfeinsitzer* or *Fokkerstaffeln*. Improved performance pointed the way to permanency and an increase in establishment. The need for such units and the lessons learned at Verdun were noted at the highest level, but a reorganization of the single-seater units to make the maximum use of their pure fighting potential had not been put into effect when the Allied offensive on the Somme broke on 1 July 1916.

The German II Army had approximately 16 single-seaters deployed in two *Kampfeinsitzer-Kommandos* (KEK *Nord* at Bertincourt and KEK *Süd* at Château Vaux) at its disposal. The Fokker E type monoplanes were completely outclassed, and although a few Fokker and Halberstadt single-seater fighter biplanes were in the area, they were at an immediate tactical disadvantage by being harnessed to the old KEK organization. The enemy had complete aerial superiority and possessed a threefold strength composed of technically superior

**20. These Albatros D Is were part of the first delivery made to Jagdstaffel 2 on Bertincourt aerodrome, September 1916. The aircraft have already been marked with the initials of the pilots' surnames to provide individual identification in the air.**

fighter aeroplanes of the Nieuport and D.H.2 type.

While the army HQ (*Armee-Ober-Kommando*) control of the *Kampfeinsitzer-Kommandos* and *Kampfeinsitzerstaffeln* had sufficed before the start of the Somme battle, the size and number of single-seater units now required, and the general increase in the number of two-seater units, could not be effectively handled by the existing organization. Intermediary controls were introduced between Army Corps or between Army Corps and the *Stofl*. These were initially known as *Fliegerleitungen*, but they were soon absorbed into the office of the *Gruppenführer der Flieger (Grufl)*. It was this officer's task to arrange the employment of the flying units allotted to or temporarily operating for Corps HQs in the best tactical way. On 21 July, II Army area south of the river Somme was designated as II Army, while the area north of the Somme was re-designated as I Army. The *Stofl* of I Army was *Hptm* Haehnelt, who had previously held the position of *Stofl* in V Army at Verdun. The number of *Kampfeinsitzer-Kommandos* in the area increased and by the end of August, I and II Armies had a combined strength of 60 single-seater fighter aeroplanes.

21. Beside his Albatros D II (386/16) Boelcke relates the details of yet another successful combat while he removes burnt powder stains from his face—a sure sign that a pilot had been in action and fired his guns.

# BIRTH OF THE JAGDSTAFFELN

The *Feldflugchef, Oberst* Hermann von der Lieth-Thomsen, gave permanency to the single-seater units when he ordered the formation of the first *Jagdstaffeln* on 10 August 1916. Despite the obvious urgency of the aerial situation on the Somme, and the fact that a single-seater element already existed within the German Air Service, operating as individual units, the introduction of these initial *Jasta* was not immediate. They were formed from cadres of experienced single-seater pilots belonging to the *Feldflieger Abteilungen* and the *Kampfgeschwadern*, many of whom were already serving with the non-permanent *Kampfeinsitzer-Kommandos* and *Kampfeinsitzerstaffeln*. In some cases an increase in establishment and a change in nomenclature were

22. Pilots of Jagdstaffel 2, November 1916: (left to right) Leutnant Sandel, Offizierstellvertreter Max Müller, Leutnant Manfred von Richthofen, Leutnant Günther, Oberleutnant Kirmaier (Staffelführer), Leutnant Hans Imelmann, Leutnant König, Leutnant Höhne, Leutnant Wortmann, Leutnant Collin.

sufficient to create a *Jagdstaffel*, but others were completely new formations. As purely offensive units, they were formed to carry out persistent attack on enemy aeroplanes and captive balloons and were intended to make it possible at any time to counter-balance the constantly increasing numerical superiority of the enemy, at least temporarily, and on any sector of the front. The main reason for their formation at this time was, of course, to attempt to overcome the air superiority of the enemy over the Somme Front.

At the end of August only single examples of both the Albatros D I and D II were at the front alongside 25 Halberstadt and 35 Fokker singleseater biplane fighters. The major part of the fighter force still comprised E category monoplanes, of which there were 124 examples at the front. It was not until the arrival of the first batches of Albatros D I and D II in number that any standardization was possible. As a result, many of the early *Jagdstaffeln* operated for the first few weeks with assorted equipment. It is considered that the lack of sufficient D category biplanes of good performance was one of the main reasons why these units took so long to become operational despite the serious aerial situation on the Somme.

We have seen how the first fighter pilots seldom had to manoeuvre in combat, but the defensive circle adopted by the F.E.2b formations when attacked and the tight-turning capabilities of the D.H.2 and Nieuport focussed attention on the need to perform '*Kurvenkampf*' tactics. Many pilots who had been successful with the Fokker monoplane could only turn in the aerodrome sense of the word, and were not capable of executing sustained tight turns without stalling, spinning or otherwise losing height. The emergence of efficient *Jagdstaffeln* was a gradual process, although even if the aircraft had been available earlier, an acute shortage of pilots skilled enough to fly them well would have presented itself. The early *Jagdstaffeln* were as follows:

## Jagdstaffel 1

The *Feldflugchef* order of 10 August laid down that *Jagdstaffel* 1 was to be formed from personnel on the strength of *Kampfeinsitzer-Kommando-Nord* with additional personnel from *Armee Flug Park* 1 and from *Feldflieger Abteilungen* within the area of I Army. The unit formed at Bertincourt under *Hptm* Zander on 22 August and moved to its first operational aerodrome at Bertigny on the 24th. Equipment included Fokker D I and D II fighter biplanes.

## Jagdstaffel 2

*Hauptmann* Boelcke was recalled from his tour of the Eastern Front by a telegram from the *Feldflugchef* on 11 August, which stated that he was to form and command *Jagdstaffel* 2. Formation began at Bertincourt on 27 August, two Fokker D biplanes and one Albatros D I (426/16) being used initially. Boelcke scored his 20th victory on Fokker D III 352/16 on 2 September and this was also the first unit victory. Six Albatros D Is were received on the 16th and as a result of enemy shelling of the aerodrome, the unit moved to Lagnicourt during the night of 22 September.

## Jagdstaffel 3

This unit had no previous organization and its formation began at *Flieger Ersatz Abteilung* 5 at Braunschweig, Germany, on receipt of the 10 August order. The *Staffelführer* was *Oblt* Kohze, who reported *Jagdstaffel* 3 ready for active service on 1 September. The unit moved to the Western Front and was initially based on Vraignes aerodrome near Péronne in I Army area.

## Jagdstaffel 4

*Oblt* Berthold, who had been the *Führer* of *Kampfeinsitzer-Kommando-Vaux*, later named *Kampfeinsitzer-Kommando-Süd*, absorbed the necessary increase in establishment of personnel and equipment from *Armee Flug Park* 2 and from *Feldflieger Abteilungen* in II Army area to form *Jagdstaffel* 4. The transformation was complete on 25 August, the unit's Halberstadt D category biplane fighters being based on the aerodrome at Château Vaux. On 1 September *Oblt* Buddecke assumed command.

## Jagdstaffel 5

One of *Hptm* Haehnelt's original *Kampfeinsitzer-Kommandos* formed for the Verdun offensive in January 1916 was based on the aerodrome at Avillers and flew for *Maasgruppe Ost* of V Army. Its personnel were initially single-seater pilots from *Kampfgeschwader* I, but during the summer some pilots from *Feldflieger Abteilungen* in the area were attached. This *Kommando*, still equipped in the main with Fokker E category monoplanes was redesignated *Jagdstaffel* 5 on 21 August under the command of *Oblt* Berr. Initially based on Bechamp aerodrome, it operated from Bellevue-Ferme aerodrome for a few days until 29 September when it moved to Gonnelieu near Cambrai in I Army area and was equipped with Halberstadt D category biplanes.

23. Vizefeldwebel Holler of Jagdstaffel 6 with his mechanics during a top overhaul on the 160hp Mercedes engine of his Albatros D II, which was probably 484/16.

24. Leutnant Leffers of Jagdstaffel 1 with a captured Nieuport 11 armed with an LMG 08/15 machine gun firing through the propeller. Leffers was shot down and killed on 27 December 1916, reputedly in this aeroplane. He was credited with nine victories, five of them having been scored on Fokker monoplanes with Feldflieger Abteilung 32.

## Jagdstaffel 6

*Fokkerstaffel-Sivry* was the result of merging the *Kronprinzstaffel (Fokkerstaffel Jametz)* with Boelcke's original *Kommando* at Sivry. After Boelcke's departure, the unit, equipped with eight obsolescent Fokker monoplanes, mostly of the E IV type, continued to operate in a stagnating aerial situation. On 25 August the designation *Jagdstaffel* 6 was given and *Ltn* Wulff named as *Staffelführer*. The forward location of Sivry had long been an inviting target and in the initial bombardment French long range guns dropped 30 high explosive shells on the aerodrome, destroying one aircraft in its tent and pitting the landing ground with craters. The ageing Fokker monoplanes were returned to *Armee Flug Park* 5 on 29 September and *Jasta* 6 moved to II Army on the Somme. Re-equipped with Albatross D I biplane fighters it occupied the aerodrome at Ugny le Quipée.

## Jagdstaffel 7

Tactically belonging to 16 Army Corps in Army Group *Kronprinz* of V Army, a *Fokkerstaffel* formed on 2 June was operating from the aerodrome at Martincourt. On 23 August this unit was given the designation *Jagdstaffel* 7 and was under the command of *Oblt* Bronsart von Schellendorf. The expansion necessary to meet the establishment laid down for a *Jagdstaffel* was not accomplished until 21 September and eight days later *Jasta* 7 moved to the aerodrome east of Senon at Bellevue-Ferme, from which *Jasta* 5 was leaving for the Somme.

Even before these original *Jagdstaffeln* were formed, an extensive increase in the number of such units was envisaged and a formation list from the *Kriegsministerium* dated 31 August mentions *Jagdstaffeln* 1 to 20. The next listing, dated 29 November, extends the upper limit to include *Jagdstaffel* 24, and this was followed a month later on 28 December with a list up to *Jagdstaffel* 36. Obviously such a programme would strain all resources to the absolute limit, and in the event it was only possible to form 25 *Jagdstaffeln* up to the end of 1916. Even this number meant that many units became operational with pilot and aeroplane strengths well below the laid-down establishment. (See Appendix I.) Some *Kampfeinsitzer-Kommandos* and *Fokkerstaffeln* had not been absorbed in the formation of the original seven *Jagdstaffeln*, but their futures did not remain uncertain for long and they were soon swallowed up in the massive reorganization that followed. Six *Kampfeinsitzer-staffeln* were formed in 1916 for the defence of important industrial areas in Germany against Allied bombing attacks. These home defence units were not used to augment the number of *Jagdstaffeln* at this time and they continued to perform their interceptor duties and retain their original designations until late in 1918.

## Jagdstaffel 8

Formed on 10 September from a nucleus of a small single-seater element in *Feldflieger Abteilung* 6 on Roulers aerodrome. The *Staffelführer* was *Hptm* Stenzel, recently returned to the Western Front from Macedonia. It is considered that a concentration of equipment and personnel occurred before the formation date since *Jagdstaffel* 8 was operational from 10 September, flying from Rumbeke aerodrome.

## Jagdstaffel 9

Following the early grouping of III Army single-seaters on the right flank of *Maasgruppe West* during the Verdun offensive, a *Fokkerstaffel* was formed at Vouziers on 1 June under *Oblt* Ascheberg and named *Armeestaffel* AOK 3. The unit was equipped with the Fokker E IV and received an increase in personnel and aircraft from 28 September when the designation *Jagdstaffel* 9 was adopted. The unit was operational in its strengthened state on 5 October 1916 flying from Leffincourt aerodrome, the *Staffelführer* being *Oblt* Student.

## Jagdstaffel 10

Although the official formation date for *Jasta* 10 is given as 28 September, the unit was in existence at least seven days earlier. It emerged from the well-known Douai-based *Kampfeinsitzer-Kommando* 3, Immelmann's old unit. Equipped with four Fokker E III, one Fokker E IV, two Fokker D II, one Halberstadt D II and two Albatros D II, it was under the command of *Oblt* Linck, and moved to Phalempin aerodrome near Lille on 25 September. By 6 October, *Jasta* 10 was operational on its new aerodrome. It was known locally as *Jagdstaffel Linck*, even after its first *Staffelführer* was killed in action on 22 October. The unit was then placed under the command of Linck's replacement, *Oblt* Volkmann.

## Jagdstaffel 11

This unit was operational from 11 October under the command of *Oblt* Lang and was based on Brayelles aerodrome at Douai. Its formation date is given as 28 September, but it was actually formed at the same time as *Jasta* 10, both of these units emerging from an amalgamation of pilots and aeroplanes from the VI Army *Kampfeinsitzer-Kommandos* 1, 2 and 3.

## Jagdstaffel 12

In VII Army area a *Fokkerstaffel West* was formed on 1 April under *Oblt* Hoenmanns, based on Paux-Fé aerodrome near Laon, and became *Jagdstaffel* 12 by increasing the establishment of aeroplanes and personnel. The war diary of the unit shows that the

Vizefeldwebel pilot, 1914–15, in Flying Troops service uniform, with branch piping in red and black. Bars on collar and cuff are branch distinctions; button and lace on collar and lace on cuff indicate rank. Plain grey shoulder-straps with red winged propeller badge and '1' of pre-war Flieger-Bataillon 1; arm patch '1' identifies Feldflieger Abteilung 1, one of eight tactical units formed by Fl.Bn.1. Pilot's badge below Iron Cross 1st Class on left breast; Iron Cross 2nd Class ribbon in buttonhole.

FOKKER E III, 103/15, of Kampfeinsitzer-Kommando Habsheim, winter 1915–16

ALBATROS D I, D.390/16, of Jagdstaffel 2, September 1916

ALBATROS D II, D.1724/16, of Kampfstaffel 11, 1916–17

OPPOSITE TOP: Fokker E III, 103/15, flown by Oblt Schild-knecht in Kampfeinsitzer-Kommando Habsheim, win-ter 1915–16. The overall beige shade is produced by clear-doping natural linen fabric. The early form of national marking is carried in the usual locations, but the serial number is applied rather further forward than normal. No individual pilot's identification is carried. The black-painted rudder and black-and-white stripes around the fuselage are markings applied to aircraft of units allocated to Armee-Abteilung-Gaede at this period.

OPPOSITE BOTTOM: Albatros D I, D.390/16, flown by Ltn Höhne in Jagdstaffel 2 during September 1916. Wings and tail are camouflaged in dark green and reddish brown on the upper surfaces, the colours meeting in a soft sprayed line. Wing and tail undersurfaces are painted light sky blue. The plywood fuselage is stained a lighter reddish-brown, and varnished; random brushed blotches of this stain are seen on the fabric rudder. Engine cowling panels and louvres, and all struts, are painted a light grey. All

national insignia are carried on square white grounds, and that on the fuselage is applied rather further forward than normal, indicating an aircraft of the initial production batch. No unit markings were carried by Jasta 2 at this time; the pilot's individual marking is an abbreviation of his name, painted on both sides of the fuselage.

ABOVE: Albatros D II, D.1724/16, flown by Ltn Schäfer in Kampfstaffel 11, Kampfgeschwader 2 during late 1916 and early 1917. The overall finish is almost identical to that of D.390/16. Following official instructions the square white grounds of the upper wing insignia were now over-painted, to leave a white border of approximately 5cm around the cross. Schäfer's individual marking is a white disc thinly outlined black, which appeared on both sides of the fuselage and the upper tail surfaces, and is echoed in the white-painted wheel covers. This temporary single-seater element was disbanded, and most of its pilots posted to Jagdstaffeln, early in 1917; Schäfer went to Jasta 11, and eventually led Jasta 28.

27

ALBATROS D III, D.629/17, of Jagdstaffel 11, May 1917

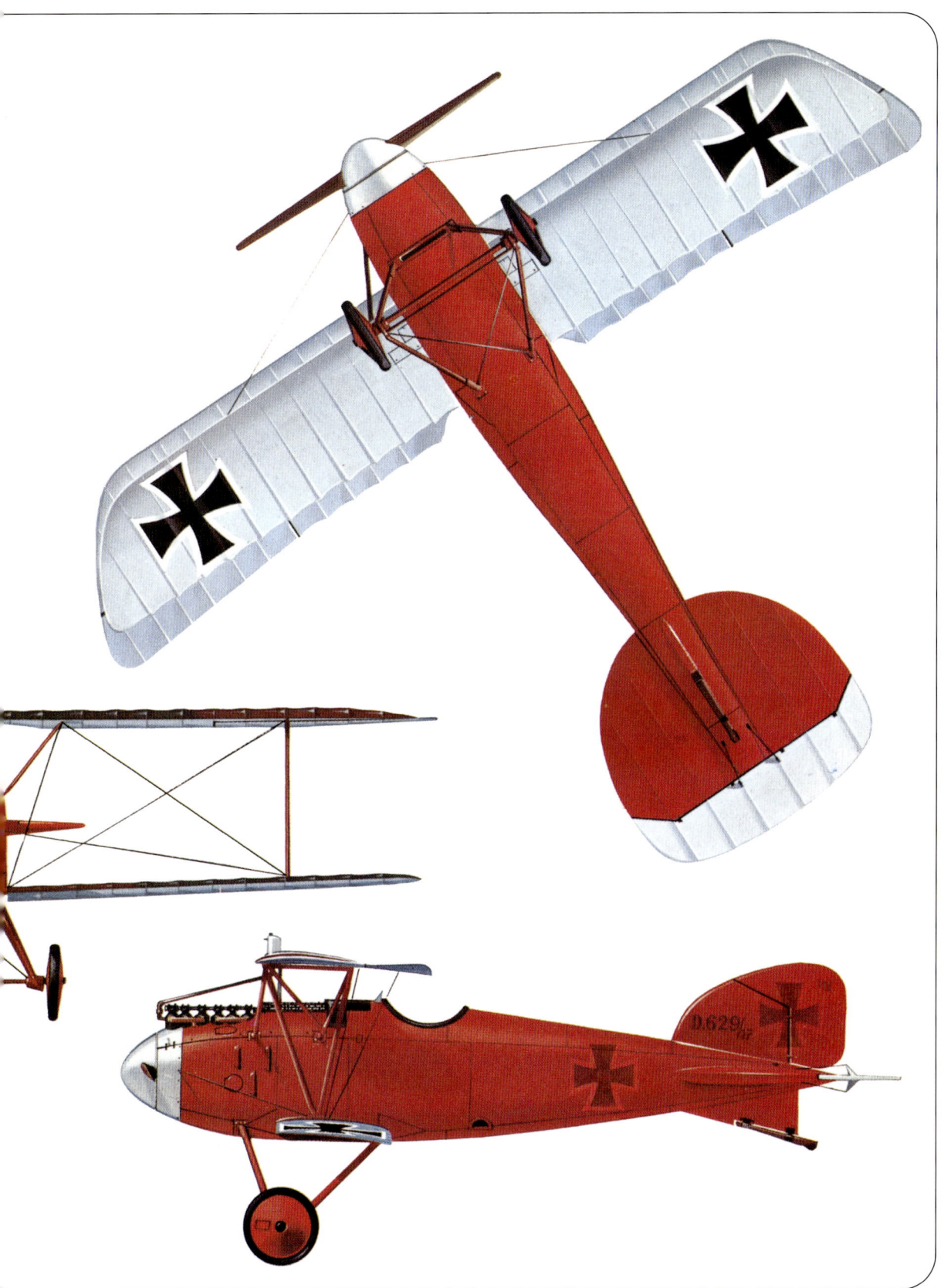

PAGES 28–29: **Albatros D III, D.629/17, flown by Ltn Karl Allmenröder in Jagdstaffel 11 during May 1917.** The finish of this machine, when delivered, was similar to previous Albatros products except that the form of national insignia had been regularized by Idflieg instructions: the 5cm white border had also come into general use. Upper surfaces of the wings were camouflaged in green and reddish brown, with light sky blue undersurfaces. Due to the increase in aerial activity at this period, units were beginning to adopt an identification marking, and the red colour which was to remain the hallmark of Jasta 11 throughout the war appears on the fuselage and tail unit of Allmenröder's machine. Note that in this case it has been applied over the national insignia and the serial number, which appear in photographs to show through the red in quite a pronounced manner.

BELOW: **Halberstadt D II, D.820/16, flown by Ltn Meier in Jagdstaffel 25 in Macedonia early in 1917.** The aircraft illustrated is one of 30 built under licence by Hannoversche Waggonfabrik A.G. (serials 800–830/16) and can be identified as such by the white-painted serial number. The finish is standard for late 1916, with upper and side surfaces sprayed in olive green and reddish-brown camouflage, and light sky blue undersurfaces. No unit marking is applied; in Jasta 25 the pilot's individual identification took the form of a letter (usually but not invariably the pilot's initial) painted on each side of the fuselage.

OPPOSITE TOP: **A selection of individual insignia:**

(A) Black 'swastika' form cross carried on all Albatros D II aircraft of Jasta 23 as a unit marking during spring 1917. This is one of the earliest examples of a Jagdstaffel unit marking, and was attributed to the fact that the Staffelführer (Hauptmann Backhaus) had previously served in a Kampfgeschwader.

(B) Three-pointed black-and-white star carried on Albatros D III D.1957/16 by Offizierstellvertreter Felsmann of Jagdstaffel 24 as an individual marking.

(C) Letter H used as an individual marking by Leutnant Henkel in Jagdstaffel 19 during spring 1917.

(D) Girl's name used as an individual marking by Leutnant Wichard of Jagdstaffel 24 on Albatros D III D.2096/16.

(E) Skull and crossbones carried on an Albatros D I of Jagdstaffel Boelcke early in 1917. This machine had its fuselage cross marked at the same location as that of D.390/16 shown in the colour plate, and although its serial number is not known, it is believed to be from the initial production batch (serial numbers 381–392/16).

OPPOSITE BOTTOM: **Jagdstaffeln had an establishment of three automobiles of which this Horch 10/30 PS Personenwagen für militärische Zwecke is an example.** Vehicles in this class were also manufactured by such firms as Adler-Werke, Benz & Cie., N.A.G., and Phänomen-Werke. The insignia refers to the service rather than to an individual unit.

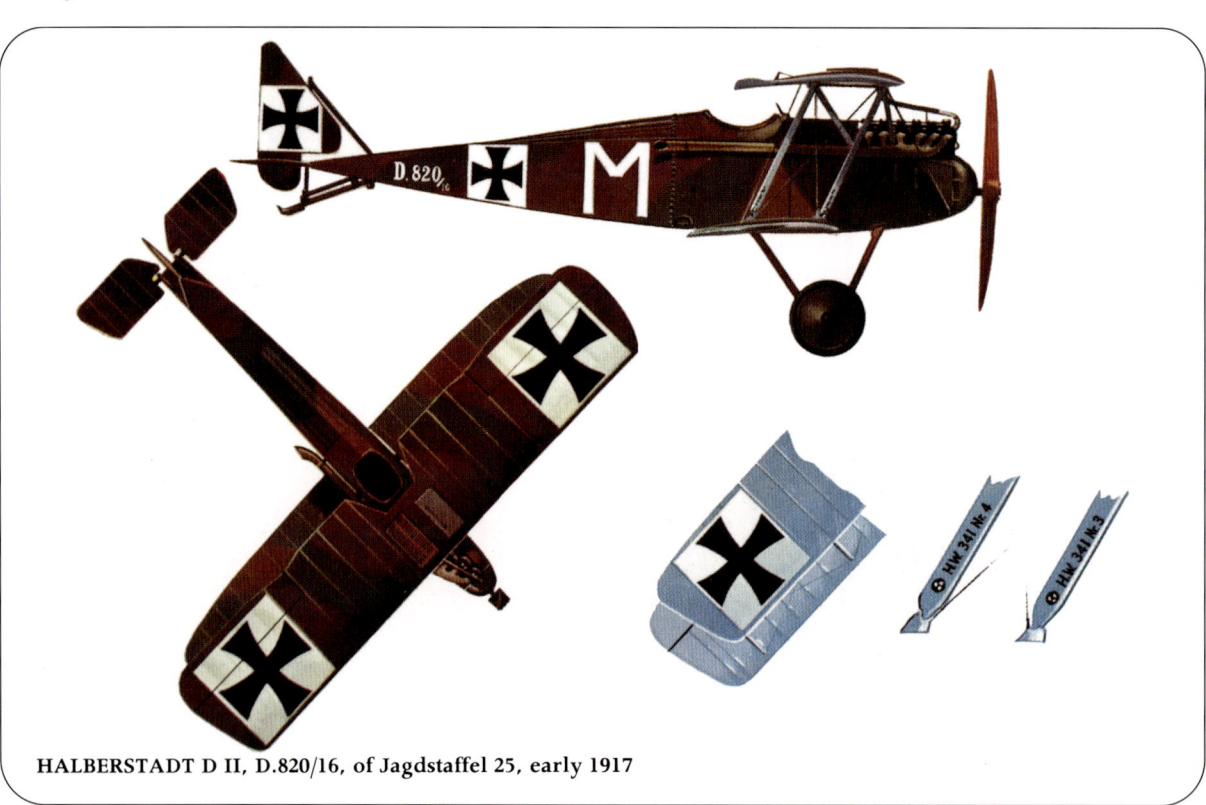

HALBERSTADT D II, D.820/16, of Jagdstaffel 25, early 1917

A

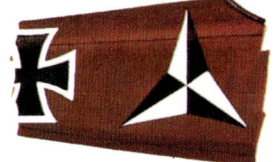

B

C

E

D

**HORCH 10/30 PS military car in Imperial Flying Service finish and insignia**

German pilot, 1915–16, in flying kit. Leather flying helmets and goggles were usually privately acquired and varied widely in details. This pilot wears a double-breasted coat, one of a number of styles of outer clothing in vogue at that time, tucked into the enormous Fliegerhosen—bulky protective trousers with eyelets for lacing up the inside leg. Flying clothes varied from pilot to pilot; many issue, private and captured items were used at whim.

Mechanic or other ground crewmen of Imperial Flying Troops in the black working uniform worn throughout the war. The cap is the normal field cap of junior enlisted ranks, with national cockades on band and crown; the black band and red piping identify the Flying Troops. Senior NCOs wore vertical bars of silver lace at front of collar each side, and peaked cap as figure on p. 25.

change in designation was first used from 6 October. The *Staffelführer* was *Hptm* von Osterroth, and the effective date of his appointment was 12 October. On 4 November, *Jasta* 12 was operational on Riencourt aerodrome in I Army area.

## Jagdstaffel 13

The date of formation is given as 28 September, although it was 22 October before *Jasta* 13 was approaching a workable establishment. It was formed by gathering the loosely dispersed single-seater pilots with the *Feldflieger Abteilungen* and *Kampfgeschwadern* in the Strantz Army Detachment area together with the *Fokkerstaffel* attached to *Feldflieger Abteilung* 19 on Porcher aerodrome.

## Jagdstaffel 14

Formed in Army Detachment A area on 28 September from the *Fokkerstaffel Falkenhausen* under *Hptm* Krieg, the unit was operational from the official date of its formation, but according to the war diary the change in designation first took place on 4 October. The unit was based on Bühl aerodrome near Saarburg and its equipment comprised two Fokker E category monoplanes, one Halberstadt D and seven Fokker D fighter biplanes. On 14 October *Oblt* Berthold was named as *Staffelführer*, replacing *Hptm* Krieg.

## Jagdstaffel 15

As early as 28 December 1915 a *Kampfeinsitzer-Kommando* existed on Habsheim aerodrome in Army Detachment B area (later Army Detachment Gaede). The official formation date for *Jagdstaffel* 15 is given as 28 September, and this is in keeping with dates given for other units formed at this time. On 3 October the first moves were taken to incorporate the changes necessary to create a permanent fighter unit, and *Oblt* Kropp was named as *Staffelführer*. On 9 October *Jagdstaffel* 15 assembled on Bixheim aerodrome, and the *Kampfeinsitzer-Kommando-Habsheim* was disbanded.

## Jagdstaffel 16

Another single-seater formation of similar standing to the *KEK-Habsheim* in Army Detachment B was *Kampfeinsitzer-Kommando-Ensisheim* based on Colmar aerodrome with *Feldflieger Abteilung* 9b. This unit was made a permanent formation from early October and was commanded by *Oblt* Dessloch, until 13 October when flying Fokker D II 528/16, he became lost and landed in Switzerland. It appears that the unit did not use the *Jagdstaffel* 16 designation until 1 November.

## Jagdstaffel 17

Formed on 23 October from *Kampfstaffel Metz*, which had been operating for the previous three months from Metz-Frescaty aerodrome on defensive duties. *Jagdstaffel* 17 emerged on 11 November under the command of *Rittmeister* von Brederlow and continued to use Frescaty aerodrome in Strantz Army Detachment area.

## Jagdstaffel 18

This unit was reported as being operational on the date of formation, 30 October. The *Staffelführer* was *Oblt* Grieffenhagen and the unit was based on Halluin aerodrome near Courtrai in IV Army area.

25. Purposeful silhouette. The Albatros D III was type tested on 26 September 1916, and 400 were ordered in October. Early in 1917 this machine reigned supreme over the Western Front and could not be produced quick enough to equip the 37 Jagdstaffeln then in existence.

26. Leutnant Fleischer of Jagdstaffel 17 flying an Albatros D II over a wintry landscape. Note that this machine is not finished in the usual camouflage scheme, but apparently has natural linen-covered wings with national insignia without the usual 5 centimetre white surround.

## Jagdstaffel 19

Formed on 25 October under *Oblt* Walz on Bühl aerodrome near Saarburg in Army Detachment A, the unit is reported to have been operational on the date of formation. Walz left on 28 November to take command of *Jasta* 2 and *Jasta* 19 was taken over by *Oblt* Hahn.

## Jagdstaffel 20

Formed via *Armee Flug Park* 2 and operational from 25 October under the command of *Oblt* Heising, the unit was based on Artemps aerodrome in II Army area.

## Jagdstaffel 21

Formation commenced at Le Chatelet on 25 October under *Hptm* von Schlieben and the unit was ready for action on 6 December on III Army front.

## Jagdstaffel 22

The order to form *Jagdstaffel* 22 was given on 25 October and on 17 November the unit assembled for the first time on Vaux aerodrome near Laon in VII Army area. Only two pilots were available, one of whom was sick; the remainder of the pilot strength had already been posted home for single-seater

training, and was not expected to return to the front before mid-December. Two Fokker D IIs left on the aerodrome by *Jasta* 12 were used initially. The *Staffelführer* was *Oblt* Hoenmanns, who had been transferred from *Jasta* 12 on 15 November. Late in December nine Halberstadt D machines were received.

## Jagdstaffel 23

Formation began on 25 October at Metz-Frescaty aerodrome in Strantz Army Detachment area. The *Staffelführer, Hptm* Backhaus, was transferred to *Jasta* 23 on 17 November from *Kampfgeschwader* 2. Completely equipped with the Albatros D II, the unit moved to its first operational aerodrome at Puxieux near Mars-la-Tour on 7 January 1917.

## Jagdstaffel 24

The date of formation is given as 25 October and work began on sheds for the aircraft on 20 November at Mörchingen aerodrome in Army Detachment A area. The *Staffelführer* was *Rittmeister* von Braun and the first actual assembly day for the unit was 1 December. Since no aeroplanes were available, five pilots were attached to *Jasta* 14 and two to *Feldflieger Abteilung* 12 for flying practice. Initial deliveries of Albatros D IIs arrived by rail at *Armee Flug Park* A and these were assembled ready for flight on 30 December.

# THE EASTERN FRONT AND BALKANS

Towards the end of 1915 three Fokker E monoplanes with pilots, mechanics and a spares holding, comprised part of an assistance programme from Germany to her Turkish ally. These aircraft were initially operated from Galata aerodrome on the Gallipoli Peninsula, and although they arrived towards the end of the campaign they were able to achieve some success in aerial combat. Amongst the victorious pilots were *Oblt* Buddecke and *Ltn* Schüz. In April 1916 the Fokkers were moved to the aerodrome at Chanak-Kale and were eventually absorbed into the Turkish *Fliegerabteilung* 6.

Buddecke, who had been decorated with the *Pour le Mérite* on 14 April, moved to Smyrna with a three aircraft element, and continued to operate there until he was recalled to the Western Front early in August to eventually take command of the newly formed *Jagdstaffel* 4. Early in 1916 *Feldflieger Abteilung* 66 was based at Hudowa in the Vardar valley, and at the end of February the first Fokker E to be sent to Macedonia was attached to this unit, being flown by *Hptm* Stenzel. With this aircraft Stenzel brought down enemy machines on 23 and 24 March. For these successes, the first aerial victories scored in Macedonia, he received written congratulations from *Gen* Mackensen. Later, when the number of single-seaters allocated to XI Army increased in number, Stenzel was given the command of a *Fokkerstaffel* formed on 1 June 1916, based on Negorci aerodrome and designated *Abwehr-Staffel-Vardar*. This unit operated with some success against the spasmodic penetrations of enemy aircraft but was forced to evacuate its

27. Leutnant Ernst Udet of Jagdstaffel 15 waits by his Albatros D III (1941/16) while mechanics Gunkelmann and Behrend work on the cooling system at Habsheim aerodrome, 1 January 1917. Despite draining the system, at very low temperatures ice formed around the vanes of the circulator pump, which necessitated flushing with hot water before replenishing the coolant for flight. The air temperature when this photograph was taken was −20 degrees Centigrade.

aerodrome on 24 August under enemy artillery fire. It was then operated for a period from Hudowa before occupying a new aerodrome near Prilep. Fokker D II single-seater biplanes now began to arrive to supplement the Fokker and Pfalz E types and on 1 October *Hptm* Burckhardt took over command from *Hptm* Stenzel, who returned to the Western Front to lead *Jagdstaffel* 8.

One pilot who served in the *Abwehr-Staffel-Vardar* was *Ltn* von Eschwege. In the reorganization of the single-seaters that took place late in 1916, he was sent further east with a detachment of *Feldflieger Abteilung* 30 to Drama aerodrome.

28. While mechanics warm up the engines of the Albatros D IIs the Staffelführer of Jagdstaffel 9 (Oberleutnant Student) briefs pilots with details of the coming patrol. The man in the centre of the group (Leutnant Junge) failed to return from this flight. The crossed swords insignia on the second machine (flown by Vizefeldwebel Köhler) shows that choice of personal markings for pilot identification was extending away from the basic letters and numerals originally used for this purpose. Note also the mudguards fitted to the undercarriages of these aircraft. Leffincourt aerodrome, 25 February 1917.

Initially flying a Fokker E III and later a Halberstadt D II, this oustanding fighter pilot ranged over 140kms of front line and was destined to score 20 victories in air combat before his death in action on 21 November 1917.

In the area of VIII Army in Russia, due to the less hectic pace of air operations and the almost complete lack of aerial opposition to reconnaissance and bombing sorties, there was little real need for single-seater aircraft. However, in keeping with the trend on the Western Front, some pilots from the two-seater *Feldflieger Abteilungen* in the east were given E category conversion courses and eventually a small number of Fokker and Pfalz monoplanes became operational in the area. It was normal to group these sparse fighter elements into *Kampfeinsitzer-Kommandos* when the tactical situation demanded. Such formations were mostly short-lived, and at the close of the operation that had caused their formation, pilots returned to their two-seater units with their aeroplanes for escort and patrol work.

## Jagdstaffel 25

The *Abwehr-Staffel-Vardar* was officially disbanded on 29 October but its remnants formed the nucleus for a new fighter formation under *Hptm* Burckhardt. Equipped with Halberstadt D II fighters it emerged one month later designated *Jagdstaffel 25*.

## Marine-Feld-Jagdstaffeln

From mid-1915 Fokker monoplanes attached to *Feldflieger Abteilungen* 40 and 33 undertook escort and defensive patrol work for the Marine Corps in IV Army area. However, late in 1915 marine landplane pilots began to undergo single-seater training at Mannheim. During 1916 the marine Fokkers were concentrated in the *II Marine Feldflieger Abteilung* at Nieumunster, and later in the year another *Kommando* existed as *I Marine Feldflieger Abteilung* based on an aerodrome near

Mariakerke. These two *Marine-Kampfeinsitzer-Kommandos* were amalgamated during the winter of 1916, and in keeping with army designations, the unit was known unofficially as the *Marine-Feld-Jagdstaffel*. This name was adopted and became official on 1 February 1917 and the formation re-equipped with Halberstadt D II and D III fighter biplanes. Albatros D IIIs were received in mid-April and selected pilots under *Ltn* zur See Sachsenberg operated them from Aertrycke aerodrome from the end of April. The pilots left at Nieumunster with the Halberstadt fighters then formed the second *Marine-Feld-Jagdstaffel* under *Oblt* Reusch.

\*     \*     \*

From the end of August 1916 the British no longer held undisputed mastery of the air over the Somme, a change in the aerial tactical situation brought about by the activities of the newly formed *Jagdstaffeln*. Formations of single-seaters forced the enemy back behind his lines and inflicted severe losses on his formations. *Hptm* Boelcke and his *Jasta* 2 were prominent in the area, scoring 21 victories in September and 30 in October. Boelcke was killed on 28 October when he crashed following a collision with *Ltn* Böhme of his own unit during a skirmish with D.H.2s from No. 24 Squadron, Royal Flying Corps.

Boelcke's contribution to the development of aerial fighting cannot easily be exaggerated; he instilled his offensive spirit in all with whom he came in contact and had been instrumental in establishing the form that permanent fighting units

should take by working closely with the office of the *Feldflugchef* at Charleville GHQ. There were of course some air-fighters who were just as skilled as Boelcke but few had the *Staffelführer's* gift of imparting fighting instruction. His teachings had a profound effect on the whole German fighter force. On 30 October *Oblt* Kirmaier became the *Staffelführer* of *Jasta* 2 and he was able to lead the unit in the Boelcke tradition, another 25 successful combats being undertaken in November.

That all the excitement of that time did not stem directly from air combat is shown by the rare experience of *Vizefeldwebel* Holler of *Jagdstaffel* 6 on 15 November 1916. This account concerns his first operational flight on the Albatros D II and also highlights the problem of orientation and the ever-present risk of becoming lost in the air. Holler had taken off at 8.06 am as the third aircraft of the first *kette*:

We had orders to climb as high as possible during the attack on Pressoir Wood scheduled for the same time. We were to protect the area from enemy reconnaissance machines. Soon after take off we flew over a continuous layer of very low cloud, I lost my bearings and followed the leader's machine, the other aircraft of our kette had disappeared earlier. At the end of the patrol time the leader gave the signal to return to base, and we both began to glide down from our height of 4,300 metres. After a short time I lost sight of the leader's machine due to my goggles becoming covered with oil. I pushed up the goggles and the oil sprayed into my eyes making the job of flying all the more difficult. I dived through the low clouds whose base was only about 60 metres above the ground, and saw a village but could not identify it. After orbiting it three times I

30. A group of pilots from Jagdstaffel 14 standing in front of one of the unit's Albatros D II aircraft on Marchais aerodrome. Left to right, Leutnants Kypke, Gröner, Michaelis, Zech, Kuen, Vonschott and Breuer.

picked a field and landed, taxying up to a tree-lined road and stopped. I retarded the ignition, switched off and took off my fur-lined boots. The oil supply pipe to the camshaft had fractured, and this had allowed the oil pump

31. Line-up of 11 Albatros D IIIs and two D IIs of Jagdstaffel 5 in front of the hangars on Boistrancourt aerodrome near Cambrai, March 1917.

to spray oil into my face. I drained the gravity fuel tank into the main fuel tank. With the aid of a piece of flexible hose from the gravity fuel line I repaired the broken oil pipe. As I was wiping the oil off my goggles, I recognized approaching troops as armed French soldiers, I was obviously down behind the French lines!

Luckily my engine had retained its compression. [The 160hp Mercedes engine was started by selecting the 'start' position on the ignition switch, retarding the ignition timing, setting the throttle slightly open and operating the hand cranking magneto.] Since I could not take off through the trees facing me, I had to turn around and took off under heavy fire that only ceased once I had entered cloud again. After flying east for 25 minutes, the repaired oil pipe began to leak again. From the air I could see Russian POWs working in the fields under German guards. I was compelled to land and found that I had come down near Hamm on the Somme. After taking off again I was forced to land once more due to my home aerodrome and the surrounding countryside being covered in thick ground fog. The place of my third landing was Ennemain and here I found that other German machines landed

behind me because of the poor weather. I eventually arrived back at my own aerodrome at 11.40.

The end of 1916 saw the fighter force rapidly becoming the elite of the German Air Service. The units already established had been born of necessity in the autumn and during the winter there was no consolidation, but an ever-increasing expansion of the force to meet the pattern agreed upon in the Hindenburg Programm. *Jagdstaffeln* 26, 27 and 28 were formed in army areas at the front, while *Jagdstaffeln* 29 to 37 were assembled at *Flieger Ersatz Abteilungen* in Germany. These units were mostly equipped with the Albatros D III, although some *Jastas* were still operating the Albatros D II, Halberstadt D III/D V and Roland D II and most were far below the required establishment in both pilots and aircraft. Their nominal strength was 12 aeroplanes, but due to the fact that some of them had so recently formed, the average actual strength was only seven machines. A special problem was the selection of officers to command these formations; the effectiveness of a *Jagdstaffel* depended greatly on the ability of the *Staffelführer* and it had already been proven that only experienced airfighters were suitable for this position. Such men when accepted were promoted to command without consideration of rank, age or seniority and it was impossible to avoid the ruthless extraction of suitable pilots from some of the elite *Jagdstaffeln* for this purpose. The *Staffelführer* of units that lost their best men in this way obviously tried to oppose the move but there was no alternative if the right men were to lead the new *Jasta*.

*Jagdstaffel* 2's contribution to the battle of the Somme in the autumn of 1916 did much more than turn the tide of aerial supremacy. Under Boelcke and his successor Kirmaier, the unit was an ideal training ground for future *Staffelführer*. Richthofen was one of Boelcke's star pupils who had been quickly entrusted with leading a *kette* in *Jasta* 2 and in January 1917 he was given the command of *Jagdstaffel* 11. Although formed out of the famous *Immelmann Kommando* at Douai this unit had no victories when Richthofen became its *Staffelführer*, but in the following three months, between 23

32. Other Ranks' canteen of Jagdstaffel 10 ready for customers.

January and 22 April it scored 100 confirmed victories, many of them falling to Richthofen himself. What *Jasta* 2 had been on the Somme, *Jasta* 11 became in Flanders, an elite fighting unit and numbering amongst its more successful pilots at this time men like Allmenröder, Schäfer and Richthofen's brother Lothar. *Jasta Boelcke* (*Jasta* 2 was so named by imperial decree on 17 December 1916) continued to produce fine fighting pilots, many of whom were later to lead *Jagdstaffeln* of

33. An Albatros D II (1742/16) of Jagdstaffel 14 marked with black and white fuselage bands, seen from inside the standard type of portable field hangar. Inside the tent can be seen a large wooden box for tools and spares and three metal containers for oil, petrol and water.

34. Readiness meant being on the aerodrome. Oberleutnant Berthold, the Staffelführer of Jagdstaffel 14 joins his pilots in an open-air breakfast at Marchais, April 1917.

It was found that the most suitable fighter aerodromes had to be as near the front as possible, with an observation post situated directly beside the standby aeroplanes. This post was continually manned and equipped with artillery types of optical measuring equipment and powerful binoculars for the observer. Telephone link with the front line observers ensured that sufficient warning was received during weather conditions when enemy aircraft approaching the front could not be seen from the aerodrome. Pilots had to be readily available somewhere near the aeroplanes, and readiness huts were essential for them to rest and relax between patrols. An alarm bell would bring the pilots to alert, and they then ran to the aircraft, whose engines had already been started by the mechanics. Only in this way could fighters be got away with a good chance of interception. Sections of at least four machines were required although six aircraft were usually used; an experienced leader was always allocated and he alone gave the order to

their own. Men such as Voss, Bernert, von Tutschek and Collin followed Richthofen in setting the highest standards and fostering the Boelcke spirit.

The selection of pilots for *Jagdstaffel* duties was now being made with more care than had attended the hasty allocation of single-seater pilots during the formation of the early *Jagdstaffeln*. A special school designated *Jagdstaffelschule* I was formed at Valenciennes on 29 November 1916, and here, pilots were instructed in formation flying and aerial fighting before proceeding to the fighter units. Some of the initial courses at Valenciennes were composed of pilots already serving with *Jagdstaffeln* at the front, it having been found that many were seriously lacking experience in formation flying and the manoeuvres necessary for effective combat use of the ever-improving single-seater machines then reaching front line units. New exponents in the art of air-fighting were beginning to emerge, and many of them were destined to proceed even further along the road of success than some of the men who had gone before. They were to follow in the tradition of Boelcke, Immelmann, Leffers, Mulzer and Parschau, all of whom had fallen in the last six months of 1916.

35. Thirteen fighter pilots had been awarded Germany's highest military decoration, the Pour le Mérite, by the beginning of April 1917. Leutnant Wilhelm Frankl, shown here, received his award on 12 August 1916 shortly before joining Jagdstaffel 4. He was killed in action on 8 April 1917 with a victory score of 19.

take off. Within the section pilots operated in pairs.

Every machine had to be easily recognized by means of a suitable marking, usually a large letter or number on the fuselage sides, while the leader's machine had a special means of recognition, often in the form of streamers. Pre-flight briefings were essential in order that pilots knew the area of intended operation and more especially that they knew where to assemble after a fight. Enemy aircraft were studied and exact methods of attack were worked out for the various types. Most were attacked from behind, some from slightly below. Basically the idea was to close up with the enemy machine as quickly as possible and only shoot when very close, throttling down when in firing position to prevent over-shooting the target.

The earlier practice of carrying out defensive patrols or barrage flights was given up in principle, being no longer considered effective. Now, a mass of single-seaters was brought into action only when the enemy was liable to appear in strength. These clashes were to be watched by the *Luftschutz Offizier* stationed well forward. The reports received by the air unit commanders at Corps HQ (*Grufl*) from these forward observation posts on weather conditions, enemy aerial activity and the general prospects for reconnaissance work, permitted the *Grufl* to form an opinion as to the advisability of sending the fighters into action.

# BLOODY APRIL

Despite the generally poor weather during the early months of 1917, aerial activity increased steadily. The newly formed *Jagdstaffeln*, although handicapped by low numbers of both pilots and aircraft, worked up to high standards of operational competence. A strategic withdrawal was made in mid-March when the German front was brought back from the Somme to the Hindenburg Line; the flying units had the difficult task of screening the operation as they themselves had to be moved without decreasing their fighting efficiency. The move was carried out under the top cover of the *Jagdstaffeln,* which in II Army area brought down

36. Mechanics of Jagdstaffel 27 bringing in the pieces of the Roland D II flown by Uffz Stein on Ghistelles aerodrome near Ghent, April 1917. This unit suffered a chronic unserviceability record with these machines and they were eventually replaced by Albatros fighters..

41

37. The Albatros D III (1954/16) flown by Leutnant Walter von Bülow in Jagdstaffel 18 being run-up on Halluin aerodrome near Menin. It was normal practice to carry out prolonged ground running and full power tests with the aircraft in flying position to ensure the correct functioning of lubricating and cooling systems.

60 Allied aeroplanes in February and March for the loss of only seven German machines. Much emphasis was placed on the use of large formations and at the end of March the *Kommandeur der Flieger (Kofl)* of II Army suggested that fighting formations composed of several *Jagdstaffeln* should be used. It was not until 30 April that machines from *Jagdstaffeln* 3, 4, 11 and 33 working for the Arras Corps at Douai were combined into one group, putting up 20 single-seaters in two formations which had several successful combats on general sweeps behind the battle area. This idea, which required a large-scale utilization of forces (in effect a reversion to patrol tactics) led to permanent and temporary groupings of *Jagdstaffeln* later in the war.

On 4 April, five days before the battle of Arras began, the British opened an air offensive, with the objective of forcing the German fighters away from the immediate battle area and allowing the army co-operation machines the greatest measure of freedom for their task. This tactic, which had worked well on the Somme, met with failure owing to the presence of well-handled German fighters, and between 4 and 8 April, 75 British aeroplanes were shot down. The hesitancy with which some of the Halberstadt and Albatros pilots had flown their aircraft earlier in the year had now disappeared. Until now the

D.H.2 had often fought the Germans with success, but from the beginning of April, the British aircraft was outclassed. The pilots of the *Jagdstaffeln* were getting the full benefit from their fine Albatros D III machines; their confidence was high and there were occasions when single machines attacked British formations—in this new period of German air superiority allied reconnaissance formations had to be given very large escorts. The low losses experienced by the *Jagdstaffeln* gave the pilots great confidence: they also had more operational experience than their British adversaries, and this, plus the excellent performance of the Albatros D III, gave them the tactical advantage in combat. The fact that an air offensive could not ensure local superiority against a determined and skilful enemy, even though he was numerically weaker, was well illustrated on numerous occasions.

The fighter units flying in support of the defensive action at Arras in April were *Jagdstaffeln* 3, 4, 11, 12, 27, 28, 30 and 33. Towards the end of April these formations had an average daily strength of only seven aeroplanes each due to losses, replacement difficulty and so on. Between 1 and 12 April there were 42 aircraft ready for action daily, and from then until the end of the month this figure had increased to 56 machines. The British estimated the strength of the German fighter force to be far higher, an error which speaks volumes for the energy and devotion to duty of the *Jasta* pilots, and for the tireless efforts of the mechanics who kept the aeroplanes serviceable. *Jagdstaffeln* working on a special operational roster were airborne up to four times a day when the tactical situation in the air was critical. The policy of strict formation grouping localized the effectiveness of the relatively small number of fighter machines and the use of the *Flugmeldedienst* service was also a major factor, since it was upon the accuracy of reports from the forward *Luftschutz Offiziere* that the *Gruppenführer der Flieger (Grufl)* evaluated the aerial situation and the opportunity to send his fighters into action. When he did so, they were required to attack the enemy not only on the German side of the lines, but whenever possible on the enemy side. That this aggressiveness was successful is shown by the large

number of aircraft brought down within the British lines.

So Bloody April, as it became known in the Royal Flying Corps, came to an end; in no other month throughout the war was the corps so hard pressed, or the casualties so heavy. No less than 362 aeroplanes and 29 balloons were brought down during the month, 299 of the aeroplanes in aerial combat, a British to German loss ratio of 4 to 1. The *Jagdstaffeln*, operating as they were at about half strength, could be proud of their success. Brought up to establishment, increased in number and operating even better aircraft, the German fighter units were certainly going to be a force to be reckoned with in the grim months ahead.

# THE AIRCRAFT

### Fokker Monoplanes

Type: Single-seat wire-braced monoplane with wing warping; fuselage and tail unit constructed from steel tube. Four main models, of which the E III was produced in most numbers:

*Wingspan* 9·52m (31ft 2¾in)    *Length* 7·2m (23ft 7½in)    *Height* 2·4m (7ft 10½in)    *Weight empty* 399kg (879lb)    *Weight loaded* 610kg (1,345lb)
*Armament* One air-cooled LMG 08/15 machine

**38. Aerodrome scene at Roucourt on 21 April 1917, showing Albatros D III machines of Jagdstaffel 11 being prepared for flight. Note the alarm bell on the tree at left.**

gun with 550rpg (E III)    *Powerplant* One 100hp 9-cylinder Oberursel U. 1 rotary (E III)
*Maximum speed* 140km/h (87mph)    *Climb rate* 1,000m (3,280ft) in 5 mins; 2,000m (6,560ft) in 15 mins; 3,000m (9,840ft) in 30 mins.

**39. Kogenluft meets the Richthofen men. General-leutnant von Hoeppner the Kommandierenden General der Luft-streitkräfte congratulating pilots of Jasta 11 on Roucourt aerodrome on 21 April 1917. Left to right: Hptm Sorg (Kofl 6), Manfred von Richthofen, von Hoeppner, Hartmann, Krefft, Schäfer, Brauneck, Lothar von Richthofen and Esser.**

**40.** Twenty Albatros D III machines lined up on Roucourt aerodrome near Douai, April 1917. The second aircraft is that flown by the Staffelführer of Jagdstaffel 11, Rittmeister Manfred Freiherr von Richthofen, and has the fuselage and tail unit over-painted in red. It is believed that aircraft from Jagdstaffeln 3, 4, 11 and 33 are included here and that this is the formation that operated with success on 30 April, making general sweeps behind the battle area for the Arras Corps.

## Halberstadt D biplanes

Type: Single-seat two-bay biplane of mainly wooden construction with steel tube tail unit and ailerons; four models built, of which the DV was the most used early in 1917:

*Wingspan* 8·8m (28ft 10½in)  *Length* 7·3m (23ft 11½in)  *Height* 2·66m (8ft 9⅛in)  *Weight empty* 561kg (1,237lb)  *Weight loaded* 771kg (1,696lb)  *Armament* One or two air-cooled LMG 08/15 MG. Aircraft usually flown with only one gun to aid performance, but provision for two with 1,300 rounds  *Powerplant* Either a 120hp Argus As.II or 120hp Mercedes D.II 6-cylinder in-line water-cooled engine  *Maximum speed* 145km/h (90mph)  *Climb rate* 1,000m in 5 mins; 2,000m in 9 mins; 3,000m in 15 mins.

## Albatros D biplanes

Type: Single-seat single-bay biplanes with semi-monocoque plywood fuselage with plywood-covered fin and tailplane; wings of wooden construction with steel tube ailerons. Rudder and elevators also of steel tube. Three models, of which the D I had a trestle type centre section, the D IIa splayed centre section struts that reduced the gap by 250mm and the D III, which was of sesquiplane layout with vee-shaped interplane struts that earned it the nickname 'Veestrutter' in the RFC.

D I: *Wingspan* 8·5m (27ft 10¾in)  *Length* 7·4m (24ft 3⅛in)  *Height* 2·95m (9ft 6⅜in)  *Weight empty* 694kg (1,530lb)  *Weight loaded* 921·5m (2,035lb)  *Armament* (all models) Twin LMG 08/15 MG with provision for 1,000 rounds  *Powerplant* (all models) One 160hp Mercedes 6-cylinder in-line water-cooled engine  *Maximum speed* 165km/h (103mph)  *Climb rate* 1,000m in 4 mins; 2,000m in 9·5 mins; 3,000m in 15 mins.

D II: *Wingspan* (as D I)  *Length* (as D I)  *Height* 2·64m (8ft 6¾in)  *Weight empty* 673kg (1,484lb)  *Weight loaded* 898kg (1,980lb)  *Maximum speed* 165km/h  *Climb rate* 1,000m in 4·84 mins; 2,000m in 9·16 mins; 3,000m in 12·66 mins.

D III: *Wingspan* 9·0m (29ft 6in)  *Length* 7·33m (24ft 0½in)  *Height* 2·90m (9ft 6in)  *Weight empty* 673kg  *weight loaded* 908kg (2,002lb)  *Maximum speed* 165km/h  *Climb rate* 1,000m in 2·5 mins; 2,000m in 6 mins; 3,000m in 11 mins.

---

## Appendix I

**The establishment of a Jagdstaffel** (as laid down in *Feldflugchef* Order 929/16, date 31/8/16)

14 Single-seater fighter aeroplanes
1 *Staffelführer*
1 Adjutant
12 Pilots
1 Paymaster
1 Master Technician
1 Disciplinary Sergeant-Major
1 Disciplinary Sergeant
1 Medical NCO
6 NCOs to include:
    1 Accountant
    1 Orderly Room Clerk
    1 for Equipment Duties
    1 for Fuel and Oil Duties
    1 for Armament Duties
    1 for General Duties
14 Engine Fitters
28 Airframe Riggers

6 Motor Mechanics
2 Electricians
2 Joiners
2 Steel Cable Workers
1 Shoemaker
2 Leather Workers
1 Tailor
2 Clerks
2 Telephone Operators
5 men for General Duties
2 Armourers
2 Motor Cyclists
15 Soldiers for Transport Duties
16 Drivers and Assistant Drivers
3 Automobiles
4 Heavy Lorries
1 Mobile Workshop
1 Water Lorry
1 Lorry fitted with Electric Generator
2 Trailers

## Appendix II

**First official victory list of German air-fighters** (*with more than three confirmed victories*)

*Dated 1 October 1916*

| *Rank* | *Name* | *Victories* |
|---|---|---|
| *Hauptmann* | Oswald Boelcke | 28 |
| *Leutnant* | Kurt Wintgens | 20 |
| *Oberleutnant* | Max Immelmann | 15 |
| *Leutnant* | Walter Höhndorf | 12 |
| *Leutnant* | Wilhelm Frankl | 11 |
| *Leutnant* | Max Mulzer | 10 |
| *Oberleutnant* | Hans Joachim Buddecke | 10 |
| *Leutnant* | Otto Parschau | 8 |
| *Oberleutnant* | Freiherr von Althaus | 8 |
| *Leutnant* | Rudolf Berthold | 8 |
| *Leutnant* | Gustav Leffers | 7 |
| *Leutnant* | Albert Dossenbach | 7 |
| *Oberleutnant* | Franz Walz | 6 |
| *Oberleutnant* | Hans Schilling | 6 |
| *Leutnant* | Wilhelm Fahlbusch | 5 |
| *Leutnant* | Hans Rosenkranz | 5 |
| *Leutnant* | Harmut Baldamus | 5 |
| *Oberleutnant* | Martin Gerlich | 4 |
| *Offizierstellvertreter* | Max Müller | 4 |
| *Hauptmann* | Martin Zander | 4 |
| *Leutnant* | Kurt Haber | 4 |
| *Leutnant* | Hermann Pfeifer | 4 |

## Appendix III

**Glossary of terms**

| | |
|---|---|
| Abteilung | Unit, detachment or section |
| Abwehr | Defence |
| Armee Flug Park | Army aviation supply depot |
| Armee Ober Kommando (AOK) | Army headquarters |
| Armeestaffel | Flying unit belonging to an army |
| Chef des Feldflugwesens (Feldflugchef) | Chief of Field Aviation |
| Eindecker-Kommando | Monoplane Detachment |
| Fähnrich | Ensign |
| Feldflieger Abteilung | Field aviation unit |
| Flieger Abteilung (A) | Aviation unit for artillery co-operation |
| Flieger | Private |
| Fliegerhosen | Flying trousers |
| Fliegertruppe | Aviation service troop |
| Flieger Ersatz Abteilung | Aviation replacement unit |
| Flugmeldedienst | Organization for reporting aerial activity |
| Fokker Gestänge Steuerung | Fokker push-rod control |
| Flugzeugmeisterei | Aircraft Technical Department |
| Generalleutnant | Lieutenant General |
| Gruppenführer der Flieger (Grufl) | Officer attached to Corps HQ responsible for the best utilization of aviation units assigned to the Corps |
| Hauptmann | Captain |
| Inspektion der Fliegertruppen (Idflieg) | Inspectorate of military aviation |
| Jagdstaffel | Fighter section or fighter unit |
| Kampfeinsitzer Abteilung | Single-seater fighter unit |
| Kampfeinsitzer Kommando | Single-seater fighter detachment |
| Kampfeinsitzerstaffel | Single-seater section |

# Appendix III contd.

| German | English |
|---|---|
| Kampfgeschwader | Fighting squadron |
| Kampfflugzeug | Fighting aeroplane |
| Kampfstaffel | Fighting section |
| Kette | Flight of three aircraft |
| Kommandeur der Flieger (Kofl) | Officer in charge of all flying units assigned to an army |
| Kommandierenden General der Luftstreitkräfte (Kogenluft) | General in command of the German Army Air Service |
| Kommando | Detachment |
| Kriegsministerium | War Ministry |
| Kurvenkampf | Air-fighting turns |
| Leutnant | Second Lieutenant |
| Leicht Maschinen Gewehr (LMG) | Light machine gun |
| Luftschutz Offizier | Air Protection Officer of the Flugmeldedienst organization |
| Nord | North |
| Oberleutnant | Lieutenant |
| Offizierstellvertreter | Warrant Officer |
| Ost | East |
| Rittmeister | Cavalry Captain |
| Sperre | Blockade |
| Stabsoffizier der Flieger (Stofl) | Staff Officer for aviation within an army area |
| Staffelführer | Leader of a section or unit |
| Staffeln | Detachments, sections or echelons |
| Süd | South |
| Vizefeldwebel | Sergeant Major |
| Werke | Works |

## Notes sur les planches en couleurs

**Page 25** : Pilote de Vizefeldwebel, 1914–15, mis en tenue de service de la Flying Troops avec tuyautage à rameau de rouge et de noir. Parement et col indiquent distinctions de rameaux et bouton et dentelle sur le col et sur le parement indiquent grade. Épaulettes grises sans dessin avec propulseur ailé rouge et Figure 1 de Flieger-Bataillon 1 d'avant-guerre ; pièce de bras '1' identifie Feldflieger Abteilung 1. Insigne de pilote dessous Iron Cross 1st Class sur sein gauche, cordon d'Iron Cross 2nd Class dans boutonnière.

**Page 26 en haut** : Fokker E III volé de Oblt Schildknecht à Kampfeinsitzer-Kommando Habsheim, hiver 1915–16. Une nuance beige total produite au moyen d'enduit clair d'étoffe de toile naturelle ; première forme de marquage national avec numéro de série plus avant que normal. Raies noires et blanches sur le fuselage et gouvernail de direction noir identifièrent un avion de l'Armee-Abteilung Gaede pendant cette période.

**Page 26 en bas** : Albatros D I volé de Ltn Höhne, Jagdstaffel 2, septembre 1916. Ailes et empennage sont peintes, le fuselage de contre-plaqué étant mis en couleur rougeâtre brun et verni ; taches de cette teinte vues sur le gouvernail de direction d'étoffe. Les insignes sur le fuselage sont plus avant que normal qui indique un avion de la première série de production. Pas de marquages de fractions furent portés par Jasta 2 à ce temps, le marquage sur le fuselage étant une abréviation du nom du pilote.

**Page 27** : Albatross D I volé de Ltn Schäfer, Kampfstaffel 11, Kampfgeschwader 2, sur la fin de 1917. À cette période une consigne eut été donnée à peindre au-dessus du fond blanc jusqu'à les insignes sur l'haute aile à l'exception d'une bordure de 5 cm. approximativement. Le marquage individuel de pilote fut un disque noir et blanc sur ailes et empennage et ceci est répété sur les enveloppes de roues. Après cette fraction provisoire fut licenciée, Schäfer alla à Jasta 11 et à la fin fut à la tete de Jasta 28.

**Pages 28–29** : Albatros D III volé de Ltn Karl Allmenröder, Jagdstaffel 11, avril 1917. D'un finis similaire aux autres avions il tient les insignes nationals revus avec la bordure étroite blanche. Action aérienne accrue amena à l'adoption des marquages d'identification desquels la rouge sur cet avion est un bon exemple ; elle indiqua Jasta 11 dans toute la guerre. Dans ce cas la couleur de Jasta a été appliquée au-dessus des insignes nationals et le numéro de série que transparaissent nettement. Le nez blanc et le gouvernail d'altitude furent les marquages personnels d'Allmenröder. Avec son dernier compte à 30, ce pilote fut abattu et tué d'un Sopwith Triplane le 27 juin 1917.

**Page 30** : Halberstadt D II volé de Ltn Meier, Jagdstaffel 25, la Macédoine tout au début de 1917. Le numéro de série peindu blanc marque ceci comme un de les 30 avions construit. 'Sous concession' de Hannoversche AG et fini total est normal sur la fin de 1916 ; le seul autre marquage fut une lettre d'identification individuelle qui fut ordinairement la lettrine du pilote.

**Page 31 en haut** : Sélection des insignes individuels (A) 'Svastika' sur Albatros D II de Jasta 23, printemps 1917 ; (B) Étoile portée d'Albatros D III de Jagdstaffel 24 ; (C) Marquage utilisé de Ltn Henkel, Jagdstaffel 19, printemps 1917 ; (D) Nom d'une fille utilisé de Ltn Wichard, Jagdstaffel 24 sur son Albatros D IIID ; (E) 'Tete de mort' sur Albatros D I, Jagdstaffel Boelcke, tout au début de 1917.

**Page 31 en bas** : Véhicule personnel pour des buts militaires avec insignes indiquants le service.

**Page 32 à gauche** : Ouvrier mécanicien mis en tenue typique noire portée d'Imperial Flying Troops pendant toute la guerre. Bande noire et tuyautage rouge identifient le rameau de service, le 'cadet à chapeau de campagne' enrola rangs.

**Page 32 à droite** : Pilote 1915–16 mis en tenue aérienne. Casque et lunettes furent ordinairement achetés à gré et ils varièrent beaucoup à l'égard de mode. Ce pilote tient un veston croisé, une de plusieures modes de vêtements extérieurs en vogue, troussé dans les Fliegerhosen, pantalons protecteurs qui tiennent oeillets pour lacer la jambe intérieure.

## Farbtafeln

**Seite 25:** Vizefeldwebelpilot, 1914–15, in Waffendienstuniform der Flying Troops mit rotem und schwarzem Waffengattungspaspel bekleidet. Manschette und Kragen bezeichnen Waffengattungsunterschiede und Knopf und Borte am Kragen bezeichnen Dienstgrad. Ungemusterte graue Epaulette mit rotem Aussenpropellor und Abbildung I des Vorkriegs-Flieger-Bataillon I; Armfleck '1' bezeichnet Feldflieger Abteilung I. Pilotsabzeichen unter Iron Cross 1st Class an linker Brust, Iron Cross 2nd Class Band in Knopfloch.

**Seite 26 oben:** Fokker E III von Oblt Schildknecht in Winter 1915–16 in Kampfeinsitzerkommando Habsheim geführt. Ein allgemeiner gelbgrauer Farbeton von klarfirnis Naturleinens hervorgezogen; frühes System Staatshoheitsabzeichen mit Seriennummer viel vorner als normal. Schwarze und weisse Streifen am Rumpf und schwarzes Leitwerk bezeichneten ein Luftfahrzeug der Armee-Abteilung Gaede während dieses Zeitraums.

**Seite 26 unten:** Albatros D I in September 1916 von Ltn Höhne, Jagdstaffel 2 geführt. Tragflächen und Rumpfende sind angestrichen, der Rumpf aus Sperrholz ist rötlich braun gefärbt und lackiert; Kleckse dieses Färbstoff werden auf dem Bespannungsleitwerk gesehen. Die Rumpfabzeichen ist mehr vorner als normal angelegt, die ein Luftfahrzeug der erste Produktionsserie bezeichnen. Keine Verbandhoheitsabzeichen wurden an diesem Zeit von Jasta 2 getragen und das Rumpfhoheitsabzeichen war eine Abkürzung des Pilorsname.

**Seite 27:** Albatros D I spät 1916 bis früh 1917 von Ltn Schäfer, Kanpfstaffel 11, Kampfgeschwader 2 geführt. Um dieser Zeitraum waren Vorschriften gegeben worden, der weisse Hintergrund bis auf die Obertragflächeabzeichen abgesehen von einer Borte ungefähr 5 Zentimeters überzustreichen. Das Einzelhoheitsabzeichen des Pilots war eine schwarze und weisse Platte auf Tragflächen und Rumpfende und auch auf den Radkappen. Nach diesem Aushilfsverband entlassen wurde, Schäfer ging ins Jasta 2 und schliesslich leitete er Jasta 28.

**Seite 28–29:** Albatros D III in April 1917 von Ltn Karl Allmenröder Jagdstaffel 11 geführt. Mit einer gleichen Oberflächengüte als andere Luftfahrzeuge besitzt es die Staatsrevisionsabzeichen mit derengen weissen Borte. Wachsender Stahltriebbetrieb ergab die Annahme Hoheitsabzeichen, deren das Rot auf diesem Luftfahrzeug ein gutes Beispiel ist. Es bezeichnete Jasta 11 den ganzen Krieg hindurch. Auf diesen Fall ist die Jastafarbe über den Nationalabzeichen und über der Seriennummer aufgetragen worden, den klar durchscheinen. Die weisse Rumpfspitze und das weisse Höhenruder waren die persönliche Hoheitsabzeichen Allmenröders. Mit seiner Schlussrechnung an 30 wurde dieser Pilot am 27 Juni 1917 mittels eines Sopwith Triplane abgeschossen und getötet.

**Seite 30:** Halberstadt D II früh 1917 von Ltn Meier Jagdstaffel 25 Mazedonien geführt. Die weisse Seriennummer bezeichnet dies als ein der 30 Luftfahrzeuge unter Lizenz von Hannoversche AG konstruiert und Gesamtoberflächengüte ist musterhaft für spät 1916. Das einzige andere Hoheitsabzeichen war ein Einzelkennbuchstabe, der gewöhnlich den Pilotsanfangbuchstabe war.

**Seite 31 oben:** Auslese einzelner Abzeichen (A) 'Hakenkreuz' Frühling 1917 auf Albatros D II der Jasta 23; (B) Stern von Albatros D III der Jagdstaffel 24 getragen; (C) Hoheitsabzeichen Frühling 1917 von Ltn Henkel, Jagdstaffel 19 benutzt; (D) Name eines Mädchens von Ltn Wichard Jagdstaffel 24 auf seinem Albatros D III D benutzt; (E) 'Kopf des Todes' früh 1917 auf Albatros D I Jagdstaffel Boelcke.

**Seite 31 unten:** Horsch 10/30 PS Personenwagen für militärische Zwecke mit Abzeichen, dem der Dienst bezeichnet.

**Seite 32 links:** Pilot 1915–16 in Fliegerschutzkleider. Mützen und Schutzbrillen wurden gewöhnlich persönlich gekauft und sie waren sehr unterschiedlich in Einzelheiten. Dieser Pilot besitzt einen zweireihigen Mantel, einen einer Anzahl Moden Aussenkleider im Schwange, in die Fliegerhosen aufgeschürzt, die Ösen besitzen, um das innere Bein zu schnüren.

## AIRWAR SERIES

### First 16 titles:

### Planned titles: